THE HANDMAID'S TALE

NOTES

including
- *Life and Background*
- *Introduction to the Novel*
- *List of Characters*
- *Time Line*
- *A Brief Synopsis*
- *Critical Commentaries*
- *Genealogy*
- *Glossaries*
- *Map*
- *Critical Essays*
  Themes
  Women in the Novel
  The Film Version
- *Review Questions and Essay Topics*
- *Selected Bibliography*

by
Mary Ellen Snodgrass, M.A.
University of North Carolina at Greensboro

WILEY

Wiley Publishing, Inc.

Editor
Gary Carey, M.A., University of Colorado

Consulting Editor
James L. Roberts, Ph.D., Department of
English, University of Nebraska

CliffsNotes™ *The Handmaid's Tale*

Published by:
Wiley Publishing, Inc.
111 River Street
Hoboken, NJ 07030-5774
www.wiley.com

Copyright © 1994 Wiley Publishing, Inc., New York, New York

ISBN: 978-0-8220-0572-8

14 13 12 11 10

1V/RV/QR/QT/IN

Published simultaneously in Canada

CONTENTS

Life and Background 5

Published Works 8

Introduction to the Novel 10

The Dystopian Novel 12

List of Characters 14

Time Line 21

A Brief Synopsis 24

Critical Commentaries 26

Genealogy 44

Map 45

Critical Essays
    Literary Analysis 67
    Literary Devices 70
    Women in *The Handmaid's Tale* 73
    Themes 75
    Setting 76
    A Note on the Film Version 78

Review Questions and Essay Topics 79

Selected Bibliography 81

THE HANDMAID'S TALE

Notes

LIFE AND BACKGROUND

The Early Years.   Margaret Atwood, one of the twentieth century's most forceful, innovative poets, novelists, and humanistic Cassandras, delights in a Connecticut relative, Mary Webster. After being hanged for witchcraft, Webster revived and escaped a second date with the noose. Such resilience and tenacity is the stuff of Atwood's fiction, as demonstrated by one of her most enigmatic characters, Offred, the resourceful, enduring heroine of Atwood's nightmarish *Handmaid's Tale* (1986). As a result of the novel's success, the author has assumed a place among science fiction writers in the wing reserved for eminent dystopians.

Margaret Eleanor "Peggy" Atwood, multitalented Canadian essayist, scriptwriter, children's author, fiction writer, and social critic, reached world-class status with the bestselling novel *The Handmaid's Tale*, a complex and disturbing futuristic thriller that placed the author among the twentieth century's leading feminist writers. The second of three children of native Nova Scotians— Margaret Killam Atwood and Carl Edmund Atwood, a forest entomologist for the Department of Agriculture—Margaret Atwood was born November 18, 1939, in Ottawa, Ontario. From infancy through most of her childhood, she and her older brother, Harold, backpacked in the north Quebec outback half the year, abandoning the city and missing weeks of school as her family took to the woods, where her father studied insects. (Atwood's sister Ruth was not born until 1951.)

At the age of six—a year before the family moved from Sault Ste. Marie and settled in Toronto in order to be nearer Carl Atwood's job on the staff of the University of Toronto—Atwood displayed her precocity by composing a self-illustrated verse series, "Rhyming Cats." To vex her free-thinking parents, she attended United Church of Canada services and dabbled in Unitarianism, Quakerism, and spiritualism.

The Atwoods, both voracious readers, stimulated their pixieish, articulate daughter's intellect without suggesting any particular outlet. Atwood read comic books, *Grimm's Fairy Tales*, Beatrix Potter classics, and the standard children's canon before attacking heavier classics, among them James Fenimore Cooper's *Leatherstocking Tales*, Sherlock Holmes' mysteries, Twain's adventure novels, Bible stories, *Robinson Crusoe, Gulliver's Travels*, and *Moby Dick*. A child of World War II, she read in her pre-teen years the war histories, *Rommel in the Desert, Mein Kampf*, and Churchill's writings as well as *Brave New World, 1984*, and *Animal Farm*. Her interest in writing, encouraged by her aunt, Ann Blades, dates to 1944, then inexplicably enters a dry period to begin again in Atwood's mid-teens, when she wrote for the Leaside High School literary magazine, *Clan Call*.

Developing the Poet's Voice. After graduating in 1957, Atwood entered Victoria College of the University of Toronto to complete a B.A. in English. She was determined to write, even though she doubted that a Canadian could succeed in the U.S.-dominated fiction market. During this fertile period, she read original verse at the Bohemian Embassy (a local coffeehouse) and penned satiric cartoons for *This Magazine* under the pseudonym Bart Gerrard. In 1961, she graduated with honors and published her first poetry collection, *Double Persephone* (1961), which earned the E.J. Pratt Medal. A Woodrow Wilson Fellow, she obtained an M.A. from Radcliffe and initiated graduate studies at Harvard from 1962–63. At the same time, she worked in market research and wrote for the CBC the libretto of composer John Beckwith's *The Trumpets of Summer*.

Serving her artistic muse compromised Atwood's unfettered lifestyle. In a mock serious article for *Ms.* magazine, she noted, "My choices were between excellence and doom on the one hand, and mediocrity and coziness on the other. I gritted my teeth, set my face to the wind, gave up double-dating, and wore horn-rims and a scowl so I would not be mistaken for a puffball." The beginning of the feminist movement in the 1960s changed her attitude toward a self-destructive mindset that she later labeled a "post-Romantic collective delusion." Atwood discovered Betty Friedan and Simone de Beauvoir and, at the same time, her own evolving poetic voice. She contributed poems and articles to *Alphabet, Blew Ointment, Acta Victoriana,* and *The Strand,* but found no outlets for a novel or for a collection of poems that remain unpublished.

For a year, Atwood taught writing and literature at the University of British Columbia, publishing a second volume of poetry, *The Circle Game* (1966), and returned to Harvard from 1965–67 on a Canada Council grant, but gave up on completing a Ph.D. and abandoned a thesis on fantasy/adventure literature. In 1967, buoyed by the Governor-General's Award and first place in the Centennial Commission Poetry Competition, she chose stability over bohemianism, married James Polk, and returned to teaching, this time at Sir George Williams University in Montreal, then for two years at the University of Alberta in Edmonton. In 1970, she took a break from her schedule of writing and teaching by touring England, France, and Italy.

Deemed a major poet by the late 1960s, Atwood returned to Toronto in 1971 to serve as York University's writer-in-residence and editor for House of Anansi Press. Her marriage to Polk ended in 1973, when she settled on an Alliston, Ontario, farm with novelist and colleague Graeme Gibson, about whom she reveals little more than that he possesses a solid ego. Atwood's literary models—all male—include Jean-Paul Sartre, Samuel Beckett, Franz Kafka, Eugène Ionesco, and Robert Graves. She also profited from the influence of critic Northrop Frye and poet Jay MacPherson, a strong female role model and friend.

A Critical Success.   From her pursuit of a demanding writing schedule, Atwood was elected chair of the Canadian Writers' Union and reaped an astounding list of awards and accolades—the Bess Hoskins Prize, Union Poetry Prize, City of Toronto Book Award, St. Lawrence Award for Fiction, Periodical Distributors of Canada Short Fiction Award, and the Canadian Bookseller's Association Award. Her most provocative novels and short stories focus on themes of exploitation and victimization. One of her children's books, *Up in the Tree* (1978), is dedicated to Eleanor Jess Atwood Gibson, her daughter, who was born in May 1976. A second book for young readers, *Anna's Pet* (1980), Atwood wrote in collaboration with Ann Blades.

Chief among Atwood's studies of people—mainly women—who refuse to be sexual or political pawns is her dystopian feminist fable, *The Handmaid's Tale*, a futuristic satire that sold over a million paperback copies in the United States alone. The novel, which has been translated into twenty languages for distribution in twenty-five countries, remained on the bestseller list for twenty-three weeks, and won her the Los Angeles Times Book Award, a second Governor-General's Award, nomination to the Ritz-Paris Hemingway Prize, and the title of *Ms.* magazine's Woman of the Year. Subsequent honors include the Arthur C. Clarke Award, Commonwealth Literature Prize, the Welsh Arts Council International Writer's Prize, and *Chatelaine* magazine's Woman of the Year. In 1990, *The Handmaid's Tale* was filmed by Cinecom Entertainment Group. The movie, scripted by Harold Pinter and set in a grim New England stronghold, features Natasha Richardson as Offred, Aidan Quinn as Nick, and Robert Duvall and Faye Dunaway as Commander Fred and Serena Joy.

In recent years, Atwood, who resides on Admiral Road on the outskirts of Toronto, continues to lecture and give public readings. Her liberal views find voice in Amnesty International, PEN, and the Canadian Civil Liberties Association, of which she served as director from 1971–73. She takes an interest in various forms of artistic expression; one of her hobbies is inscribing greeting cards with rhymed verse. Continuing her balanced production of prose and poetry, in 1992, she published *Good Bones*, a collection of verse, essays, and short fiction, and in 1993, the bestselling novel *The Robber Bride*. A current resident outside Alliston, Ontario, she remains active in women's issues and literary circles, particularly the Canadian Authors Association. A respectable collection of Atwood criticism resides in the Robarts Library at the University of Toronto. Her manuscripts are collected at the university's Thomas Fisher Rare Book Library. A Margaret Atwood Society thrives in the U.S., fueled by studies in feminism and fiction.

PUBLISHED WORKS

drama
The Servant Girl, 1974

novels
The Edible Woman, 1969
Surfacing, 1972
Lady Oracle, 1976
Life Before Man, 1979
Bodily Harm, 1981
Encounters with the Element Man, 1982
Murder in the Dark, 1983
Unearthing Suite, 1983
The Handmaid's Tale, 1985
The Robber Bride, 1993

juvenile fiction
Up in the Tree, self-illustrated, with Joyce C. Barkhouse, 1978
Anna's Pet, with Ann Blades, 1980

poetry
Double Persephone, 1961
The Trumpets of Summer (libretto), 1964
The Circle Game, 1966
The Animals in That Country, 1968
The Journals of Susanna Moodie, 1970
*How Do I Love Thee: Sixty Poets of Canada and Quebec Select and
    Introduce Their Favourite Poems from Their Own Work*, 1970
Five Modern Canadian Poets, 1970
Procedures for Underground, 1970
Power Politics, 1971
You Are Happy, 1974
Selected Poems, 1976
Two-Headed Poems, 1978
True Stories, 1981
Snake Poems, 1983
Interlunar, 1984
Selected Poems II, 1986

short stories
New Canadian Stories, 1972
"Hair Jewelry," *Ms.*, December 1976
Bluebeard's Egg, 1983
"Poppies," *Saturday Night*, November 1992
Dancing Girls and Other Stories, 1993

Wilderness Tips, 1993
Likely Stories: A Postmodern Sampler, 1993

mixed collection
Good Bones, 1992

history
Days of the Rebels: 1815–1840, 1977

criticism
Survival: A Thematic Guide to Canadian Literature, 1972
Canadian Imagination: Dimensions of a Literary Culture, 1977
To See Our World, with Catherine M. Young, 1979
Second Words: Selected Critical Prose, 1982

editing
The CanLit Foodbook, 1987
The New Oxford Book of Canadian Verse in English, 1982
The Oxford Book of Canadian Short Stories in English, 1986
The Rushdie Letters: Freedom to Speak, Freedom to Write, with
    Robert Weaver, 1993

disc recordings
The Poetry and Voice of Margaret Atwood, Caedmon, 1978

INTRODUCTION TO THE NOVEL

In an interview for *The Progressive,* Margaret Atwood explains
how she came to write *The Handmaid's Tale,* which is often labeled
speculative fiction because it appears to predict or warn of a triumph of totalitarianism or what one reviewer calls a "Western
Hemisphere Iran." Having absorbed the New England Puritan tradition during her studies at Harvard, she observed the rise of the U.S.
political right in the 1980s and compared the Moral Majority's
grass-roots menace to the phenomenon of Hitler. According to
Atwood, the Nazi leader told the world what he intended to do; then
he set about accomplishing his heinous aims. The ranting diatribes
of late twentieth-century American right-wingers, who steadfastly
push women back into the traditional roles common in the 1950s,
delight in the AIDS epidemic among homosexuals, and threaten
death to members of the gay culture, parallel Hitler's fascist candor.
Atwood claims to have acted on a what-if scenario: suppose ultra-

conservatives did achieve a coup d'état and turned rhetoric into a stringent authoritarianism, replete with suspension of constitutional rights, racial cleansing, torture, perpetual sectarian wars, public execution of homosexuals and dissidents, a repressive police and spy operation, and assignment of roles to women based on their childbearing capabilities.

So trenchant and compelling is Atwood's fictional premise that critics were bound to clash in their individual responses and interpretations. During the months following publication of the novel and a parallel period after the release of the film version, a variety of voices filled columns and reviews with their responses:

• Barbara Holliday, writing for the Detroit *Free Press*, granted the novel the adulation due a "brilliant and Machiavellian" thriller, but noted plot shortcuts, particularly the President's Day massacre of the U.S. president and the Congress, who are machine-gunned in one neat guerrilla attack. Holliday labels this unlikely scenario "a coup in a Banana Republic."

• Doris Grumbach, reviewing for the Chicago *Tribune*, strikes to the heart of Atwood's purpose—shocking the audience with her dystopian view, which is "gripping in its horrendous details, striking in the extensions Atwood makes from what is true now of our society to what might possibly be true in time to come."

• From a strictly literary perspective, John S. Nelson, writing for the Wichita, Kansas, *Eagle-Beacon*, pegs *The Handmaid's Tale* as a "cross between *1984* and *The Scarlet Letter*," an oft-repeated duo of comparatives that draw on themes of religious authoritarianism, repression, indoctrination, treachery, and victimization of women.

• A pointed complaint of Robert I. Davis' review for the Greenburg, Pennsylvania, *Tribune* is the limited development of characters, both male and female. Other critics lament that the Commander and Nick receive so little fleshing out, particularly during the evening at Jezebel's and on the evening of Offred's arrest.

• Elliot Krieger, book editor for the Providence, Rhode Island, *Journal*, brings Atwood up short for misinterpreting American devotion to free thought and speech. In what Krieger refers to as Atwood's ludicrous overestimation of ultra-right clout, Americans appear to roll over and play dead, demonstrating an unreal tendency to be "sheepish, malleable, easily duped." Krieger concludes that Atwood intends not so much to warn as to ponder the ramifications of the "so-called return to traditional values."

• Alix Madrigal, a staff writer for the San Francisco *Chronicle*, who interviewed Atwood during her visit to the newspaper's office, claims that the fictional regime in Gilead lacks cohesion because its Christians and its revolutionaries express too little fervor, too little devotion to God or leaders. He concludes: "With no unifying vision, the center doesn't hold."

• Paul Skenazy, a literature teacher reviewing for the San Jose, California, *Mercury News*, lauds Atwood, but criticizes the novel's ending—the Twelfth Symposium on Gileadean Studies set at the University of Denay, Nunavit, on June 25, 2195—as "inept." He says, "It is Atwood at her cutest and most unappealing, a jarring piece of narrative silliness that adds little one could not already guess."

• More laudatory is Cathy Warren, an author reviewing for the Charlotte, North Carolina, *Observer*, who depicts Atwood's work as "the cry of a female Jeremiah. . . . *The Handmaid's Tale* is not a feminist novel; it is a political one in the Orwell tradition. It is a savage and gripping book, the kind you wish you could put aside but can't."

Atwood herself feared that readers would label her paranoid, but out of alarm at the growing power of anti-abortion terrorism and repressive, anti-female religio-political groups, she continued collecting ominous news clippings from the United States, Romania, Russia, Iran, and South Africa to use during the writing of *The Handmaid's Tale.* She noted: "I sometimes wake up in the night with disturbing thoughts. . . . What if this book is not a warning, but a forecast?" North American parallels to her thoughts were revealing: Canadian readers worried that such a reactionary cabal *might* form; U.S. readers shuddered in dread that a right-wing dictatorship was not a matter of *if* but *when.*

THE DYSTOPIAN NOVEL

As Atwood reveals through her essays and interviews, *The Handmaid's Tale* is an outgrowth of the twentieth-century dystopian **point of view.** Unlike pre-twentieth-century dreamers, altruists, and sectarians—such as Bronson Alcott, Robert Owens, Henry David Thoreau, Mother Ann Lee, Joseph Smith and Brigham Young, Mary Baker Eddy, and Charles Fourier, who created perfect worlds on paper and launched experimental utopias (for example, Brooke Farm, Pennsylvania Dutch enclaves, Christian Scientists' Massachusetts Metaphysical College and Pleasant View Home, the pioneer beginnings of Salt Lake City, Utah, and the New Harmony and Oneida communes), dystopian writers countered unbridled idealism with a worst-case perspective. George Orwell, master of the genre, wrote *1984* (1949), a nightmare novel set in London under a totalitarian regime where manipulative rewriters of history change facts to suit political exigency, manipulate language to serve the truth of the moment, and suborn party menials with threats, coercion, and subtle terrors. Orwell's brief beast fable, *Animal Farm* (1945), presents a similar controlled misery in miniature as the disgruntled animals on an English farm revolt and evolve a fascist pig-run police state, which is far worse than their former servitude to the human farmer.

Other anti-utopian classics from the twentieth century exhibit the doubts, fears, and discontent of notable dystopists: Ayn Rand (*Anthem*), Aldous Huxley (*Brave New World*), Anthony Burgess (*A Clockwork Orange*), Karel Capek (*R.U.R.*), and Ray Bradbury ("There Will Come Soft Rains" and *Fahrenheit 451*).

In most instances, creators of these hell-on-earth visions draw on the perversion of science and technology as a major determinant of society's function and control. For example, Bradbury's *Fahrenheit 451* is set in a California dystopia which features a fire department whose sole purpose is book-burning. Likewise, Aldous Huxley's *Brave New World* contains a baby factory capable of manufacturing the prescribed number of people in each of five intellectual levels and indoctrination centers that train the resultant infants to embrace their lot in life. In contrast to the technical wizardry of Capek, Burgess, Bradbury, and Orwell, Rand, in *Anthem*, evolves a society in which innovation is suppressed and people are forced to live in primitive squalor.

Atwood, whose *Handmaid's Tale* demonstrates elements inherent in the dystopian genre, echoes numerous motifs and literary devices. Like Huxley's creation of a drug-calmed society, her characters awaiting execution appear tranquilized by shots or pills. Like Huxley's engineered reproduction, Atwood's fictional Gilead depends on the allotment of enslaved babymakers as a means of assuring the birth of white children to repopulate a declining Caucasian nation. A factor that Atwood's novel shares with Rand's *Anthem* and Orwell's *Animal Farm* is the subversion of aphorism as a means of indoctrination. Further enforced by overseers, these simplistic precepts are subject to change or reinterpretation, depending on the exigencies of the artificial society which they are meant to bolster and legitimize.

LIST OF CHARACTERS

Offred

This unidentified, faithful wife of Luke, mother of a daughter, and successful clerk or computer operator working in the discing room of an office or possibly a library among eight or ten other female employees, bears the state-contrived label of "Offred," a term that identifies her as a handmaid specifically to be bred "by Fred." Early in the novel, before she has become "Offred," she is separated from work and loses control of her finances, feels the stirrings of paranoia, and agrees to attempt flight across the Canadian border. The failure of her family's escape leaves her uncertain as to the safety and disposition of family members, who may still survive in the society of Gilead. After becoming the psychologically conditioned Handmaid and mistress of Commander Frederick, she fails her state-mandated mission—to conceive a child.

Agreeing to the urging of Serena Joy, Offred becomes the lover of Nick, the family chauffeur. At Nick's instigation, Offred flees with double agents posing as the secret police. Evidence suggests that she departed the Boston area via the Underground Female-road, settled in a Quaker way station in Bangor, Maine, and taped a narrative about her servitude in Gilead. Like other escapees, Offred may have relocated in Canada or England, possibly to live in seclusion.

Moira

A next-door friend to the novel's central character during college, Moira, who shares internment at the Rachel and Leah Re-Education Center, remains "quirky, jaunty, athletic . . . irreverent, resourceful." She organizes an "underwhore party" to sell risque lingerie to college girls, and later she works for the publishing division of a women's collective. After the takeover of the Congress and suspension of the Constitution, Moira warns her friend that something bad will happen.

A logical, skillful survivalist, after being remanded to Handmaid training, she lifts Offred's spirits in clandestine meetings in the washroom. Moira suffers torture for feigning an attack of appendicitis, then overpowers a matron and escapes. Reunited with Offred, Moira continues their tradition of washroom conspiracies at Jezebel's, a nightclub where Moira works as a prostitute. Moira, who is happy to coexist among other lesbians, explains how she was remanded there because of her incorrigible behavior. After Offred's only visit to the night spot, she learns no more about Moira's fate.

Serena Joy

A former soprano on the *Growing Souls Gospel Hour* and crusader for traditional female roles, Serena Joy, whose real name is Pam, once performed maudlin TV antics; she was well-known for being able to weep copiously on camera. Serena enters late middle age with arthritis and the responsibilities of the Commander's household. Pampered by servants, she putters about her garden, sometimes just sitting under a willow tree or leaning on her cane in contemplation of her flower beds. A barren Wife, she detests the intrusion of the Handmaids, who threaten the stability of her marriage. On June 25, 2195, Professor Pieixoto believes that he has possibly identified her: she could be Thelma Waterford, wife of Frederick R. Waterford.

The Commander

A gray-haired former market researcher and semiretired top military official of the Eyes, his sober posture and stooped shoulders give away his age. Mild-mannered, but cynical and acquisitive, he rules over Wife and Handmaid as though they are chattel and interprets the ban on pre-Gilead decadence as it suits his needs and desires. After the Commander gets to know Offred, he treats her like a precocious child or lap dog and takes pride in her skill at Scrabble. She sees him as "daddyish" and recognizes his loneliness and need for heavy nighttime drinking.

Tentatively identified by historians as either Frederick R. Waterford or B. Frederick Judd, Professor Pieixoto's description seemingly pinpoints the former as Offred's mate. Waterford was the designer of the Handmaids' uniforms and originator of the term "Particicution." He succumbed to a political purge as a direct result of his "liberal tendencies" for retaining banned pictures and books and for "harboring a subversive."

Nick

A trusted, over-confident chauffeur for the Commander, he bears messages that summon Offred to the office and supplies black market cigarettes to Serena Joy. When Offred first enters the Commander's household, she notices Nick, who is polishing the staff car; soon afterward, he regularly stares at her, shows off his muscles, whistles, and displays an insouciant cockiness that belies his later importance in her life. As Offred's lover, Nick listens dispassionately to her recital of past history and emotional outpourings during their fervid lovemaking. On the day that Serena confronts Offred with evidence of adultery and calls her a slut, Nick, purportedly an operative for the Eyes and double agent for Mayday, sets up a phony arrest and has her spirited away in an Eyes van, possibly to an Underground Femaleroad way station in Bangor, Maine.

Aunt Lydia

Caught up in her fervency as a vigilant matron at the Rachel and Leah Re-Education Center, Lydia, with her uplifted face, protruding yellow teeth, and steel-rimmed spectacles, spouts a tedious line of platitudes and truisms, warnings against immodesty, materialism, and a lack of interest in the traditional maternal role, especially motherhood. She seems sincere in her belief that the "Republic of Gilead . . . knows no bounds. Gilead is within you."

Like a glory-struck drill sergeant, Aunt Lydia, armed with pointer, whistle, and cattle prod, stalks the gymnasium/barracks and administers mild, authoritative taps, a demonstration that "a little pain cleans out the mind." In class, she inculcates Gilead's future Handmaids with simplistic dogma: "It's a risk you're taking . . . but you are the shock troops, you will march out in advance, into dangerous territory. The greater the risk the greater the glory."

Luke

Offred's husband is recalled in wisps of memory—the two of them walking down the street as they discussed buying a house or starting a family, throwing out accumulated plastic grocery bags to protect their daughter from suffocation, making up the term "sororize" to mean "acting like a sister." After fleeing his first wife to rendezvous with the novel's main character during afternoons in hotel rooms, he enjoys lying close with her. A good-natured man, Luke teases his feminist mother-in-law about the differences between men and women. She refers to him as a chauvinist "piglet."

After the creation of the despotic state of Gilead, Luke exhibits what his wife interprets as paternalistic attitudes and behaviors toward her disenfranchisement and impounded bank account. He devises an escape plan and helps ease her tensions as the family packs a picnic and drives leisurely toward the Canadian border. Gunshots indicate that the foiled escape may have caused his death or, at best, grave injury during his capture.

Ofglen

The second of three Handmaids "of Glen" during the story, this current Ofglen serves as a daily shopping companion for Offred three weeks after her arrival at the Commander's house. Giving the impression of exhibitionistic piety, Ofglen asks to divert their return from town so that she can pray at the churchyard. Later, Ofglen reveals that her sanctimony is pretense, a cover-up for "us," an ill-defined rebel group. A rabid participant at the Salvaging, Ofglen, a target of the Eyes, hangs herself before she can be arrested. Her replacement becomes the novel's third Ofglen.

Rita

Serena Joy's tight-lipped, over-sixty kitchen servant frowns at Offred and rifles officiously through the groceries in her basket. Rita, who envies Offred her freedom to walk to the market, exerts limited domestic power by unlocking a cupboard and parceling out a single kitchen match to Offred.

Cora

Serena Joy's fiftyish cleaning woman discovered Offred's predecessor hanging from the bedroom light fixture and later finds Offred sleeping in the closet and fears a subsequent suicide. A childless, dull-witted drone, Cora offers the semblance of friendship to Offred by concealing an untouched breakfast. Out of frustration for the family's lack of children, Cora weeps as Offred is led away.

Offred and Luke's Daughter

A small girl, she is only a sweet, ephemeral memory of Offred's past. The child was kidnapped briefly from a shopping cart one Saturday when she was eleven months old. Offred and the child were separated when the child was five. A single Polaroid picture confirms that she survived capture and is being groomed as a white-gowned Daughter.

Offred's Mother

An ardently militant feminist, she gave birth to her daughter at age thirty-seven and would be seventy at the time of the story, if she survived. Offred's mother maintained a platonic relationship with her mate and engaged in harmless badinage with son-in-law Luke, but was in deadly earnest on the Saturday when her companions burned pornographic magazines in the park. In Offred's dim memories, after a pro-feminist balloon release, her mother fades into the crowd as though losing her identity in mob mentality. At the time of the takeover, she lives in Boston and makes frequent visits to Offred's residence. Moira recognizes Offred's mother as an Unwoman in a documentary film about the nuclear-polluted Colonies, where the life span of clean-up crew members averages three years.

Janine/Ofwarren

A former waitress, mother, and fellow Handmaid-in-training with Moira and Offred, she loses herself in the "ecstasy of abasement" and consults privately in Aunt Lydia's quarters. Before other inmates at the Red Center, Janine testifies publicly to gang rape during the decadent period preceding the formation of Gilead. Her trance-like state alerts Moira and Offred to her tenuous hold on reality. Aunt Lydia rebukes Janine for maudlin displays of piety, but calls on her to spy among the other girls for information concerning Moira's escape.

In later encounters, Offred observes Ofwarren's self-important display of a rounded abdomen during the late months of pregnancy, a violation of rules protecting expectant mothers from unnecessary public exposure to injury or harm. After the birth of baby Angela, Ofwarren weeps "burnt-out miserable tears." Her triumphant delivery of a healthy child assures that she will never be sent to the Colonies or declared an Unwoman. Later, the baby proves to be a "shredder," a failure that Janine blames on herself. During the Particicution, Janine, her eyes denoting madness, benignly smiles at the savagery she participates in.

Aunt Elizabeth

A key authority figure at the Red Center, she guards the washroom on the day of Moira's escape. Although Aunt Elizabeth suffers assault, stripping, feet-to-neck trussing, and confinement behind the furnace for seven hours, the authorities treat her as a possible collaborator by conducting an official interrogation. As birth master, Aunt Elizabeth supervises Ofwarren during childbirth and smiles as she delivers baby Angela.

Delores

She is a Handmaid-in-training who wets the floor rather than leave an afternoon session of Testifying.

Offred's Predecessor

The Handmaid who previously occupied Offred's room, she visited the Commander in his den, accompanied him to the club, and scratched a **doggerel** Latin phrase in the closet. Serena's discovery of the illicit affair led to the former Offred's suicide and the removal of the bedroom light fixture from which she hanged herself. The current Offred, who ponders the personality and fate of the doomed Handmaid, calls her "my ancestress, my double."

Ofcharles

She is a Handmaid who is executed for an unnamed crime at a

Salvaging during the summer of Offred's third year at the Commander's house.

Alma

A Handmaid who whispers her real name to Offred during the birthing ceremony, she offers to report any clues about Moira's whereabouts. Offred suppresses the urge to ask about Luke, whom Alma would have no reason to know.

Professor Maryann Crescent Moon

She is a glib, mildly humorous chair of the Twelfth Symposium on Gileadean Studies and a professor at the Department of Caucasian Anthropology at the University of Denay, Nunavit, a fictional setting in the Arctic region.

Professor James Darcy Pieixoto

The tediously pedantic director of the 20th and 21st Century Archives at Cambridge University, England, he serves as keynote speaker at the Twelfth Symposium on Gileadean Studies.

Wilfred Limpkin

A sociobiologist during the early Gileadean period, he was present at meetings of the Sons of Jacob Think Tank. Limpkin kept a diary in code and, foreseeing his demise, hid it with his sister-in-law in Calgary. His interest in "the odder practices of the regime" produce documents that convince him that Offred was Handmaid to Commander Frederick R. Waterford.

Frederick Judd

According to Limpkin's diaries, Judd was a "hard-liner" Commander of the Eyes from Gilead's early period and was responsible for banning literacy for women. He masterminded the President's Day Massacre as well as the National Homelands and Jewish boatperson plans and used scapegoating through Particicution as a relief of tensions among Handmaids.

TIME LINE

Offred's birth (mid-1950s)	Offred's thirty-seven-year-old feminist mother disdains her mate, a useless man with memorable blue eyes who lives on the coast.
late 1950s	At age four, Offred receives a pop-up book of reproductive organs. A year later, Offred and her mother attend a Saturday rally and pornographic magazine burning in the park. A participant gives Offred a magazine to burn.
late 1960s	At age fourteen or fifteen, Offred resents the illegal activities of her mother and other radical feminists.
mid-1970s	During their college years, Offred and Moira become friends.
late 1970s	Before Luke's divorce, he and Offred enjoy a premarital affair and meet in a hotel for afternoon trysts. During Offred's pregnancy, she and Luke lie in bed and monitor their unborn child's movements.
early to mid-1980s	In September of Offred's daughter's third or fourth year, repressive measures halt Pornomarts, Feels on Wheels, and Bun-Dle Buggies and cancel Offred's Compunumber. These events, prefaced by the President's Day Massacre and suspension of the Constitution, comprise a hostile fundamentalist takeover—the beginning of early Gilead.
2:00 P.M. the next day	Offred and other women are fired from their jobs. Offred's mother disappears.
mid-1980s	In September of Offred's daughter's fifth year, Luke, Offred, and the child attempt to flee Gilead and cross the Canadian border. Offred and the child run through the woods and are apprehended and separated by unidentified pursuers. Luke's fate is unknown.

two weeks after Offred's placement at the Rachel and Leah Re-Education Center	Janine is ridiculed as a crybaby. Offred willingly takes part in the ritual of public humiliation.
a week later	The authorities bring Moira to the Center for Handmaid indoctrination. Bruises suggest that she resisted arrest.
four days later	Moira and Offred make tentative contact and arrange a meeting in the end stall of the washroom at 2:30 P.M.
2:30 P.M.	Janine allows a group session to turn her testimony of gang rape at age fourteen into a unanimous accusation of seduction and criminality for having an abortion. Janine claims to have deserved the pain.
late winter or early spring of Offred's thirty-third year	After service to a bald-haired man, Offred is reassigned to the Commander.
three days later	Offred discovers a Latin inscription scratched into a closet wall by the former Offred.
three weeks after arrival at the Commander's home	Offred's Handmaid companion disappears; a second Ofglen takes her place.
May	Offred discovers the Commander snooping near her room. She undergoes a mating ceremony and returns to the sitting room to steal something. Nick interrupts her and informs her that the Commander wants to see her the next night.
the next day	Ofwarren gives birth to Angela. At nine o'clock that evening, Offred goes to the Commander's office and plays Scrabble. Back in her room, she fights hysteria and sleeps in the closet.

the next morning	Cora finds Offred in the closet and fears she has committed suicide.
end of the first year	Offred observes her first Salvaging.
July of Offred's third year at the Commander's house	Offred takes part in a Prayvaganza and joins the Commander at the nightclub, where she reunites with Moira for the last time. Moira divulges that Offred's mother, an Unwoman, works in the Colonies. Offred and the Commander take a room, where they have intercourse. After midnight, Offred, returned to the Commander's house, follows Serena through the dark kitchen and out to Nick's quarters for forbidden sex.
high summer	Offred takes part in a Salvaging, where three women are hanged and a man is torn to bits. That afternoon, the second Ofglen is replaced by a new Ofglen, who divulges that her predecessor hanged herself after seeing the van coming for her. Serena stops Offred at the steps and accuses her of sluttish behavior with the Commander.
that night	Nick bursts into Offred's room and urges her to accompany two men in a black van. The Commander objects and is, according to a twenty-second-century scholar's theory, later executed for harboring a subversive (Nick).
middle Gilead	Authorities grow more cautious about liberalism.
June 25, 2195	At the Twelfth Symposium on Gileadean Studies, Professor James Darcy Pieixoto, a British archivist from Cambridge University, explains how Offred's cassette tapes were unearthed in Bangor, Maine, and pieced together into a puzzling and incomplete retelling of her ordeal.

A BRIEF SYNOPSIS

In the mid-1980s near Boston, Massachusetts, a cabal of right-wing fundamentalists murders the U.S. President and members of Congress, disenfranchises women by impounding their credit cards and denying them jobs and education, and sets up Gilead, a repressively conservative state bent on annihilating homosexuals, abortionists, and religious sects other than their own, and resettling Jews, old women, and nonwhite people in radioactive territory, known as the Colonies. Because nuclear and biological warfare has polluted vast areas, the population suffers a sharp decline in viable births and a rise in birth defects. Consequently, infertile and aged females, as well as homosexuals, are dispatched as clean-up crews in the Colonies. Fertile women involved in illicit liaisons or second marriages are apprehended, indoctrinated, and parcelled out to Commanders of the secret police as Handmaids. These reduniformed breeders live in seclusion and virtual slavery and are deprived of their real names and labeled with a patronym of the men who control their lives—as in "Ofcharles" and "Ofwarren." The purpose of these polygynous relationships is the perpetuation of the white race, which carries on warfare in outlying areas in a struggle for supremacy.

Offred, the second wife of Luke and mother of a five-year-old daughter, attempts to escape to Canada. She is apprehended and separated from her family. Her mother, a vocal feminist, disappears. Virtually alone and friendless, Offred is selected as a potential breeder and indoctrinated at the Rachel and Leah Re-Education Center. The Handmaids-in-training share pared-down barracks-like quarters in a gymnasium surrounded by fences topped by barbed wire. Reunited with her feisty, rebellious college pal Moira, Offred maintains spunk and individuality while pretending to follow the direction of sadistic armed matrons, particularly Aunt Lydia and Aunt Elizabeth.

After lights out, Moira, Offred, and other Handmaids offer surreptitious support, survival tips, and bits of information. Like conspirators, they observe the patrolling Aunts and seize unguarded moments for normal behavior, including gripe sessions, food stolen from the cafeteria, and brief touches of hands between cots. Janine, a compliant stooge, struggles so hard to adapt to the restrictive Handmaid lifestyle that she retreats into a blank stare, evidence of impending mental and emotional collapse. Because Moira pretends to suffer an attack of appendicitis, she is tortured by beatings with steel cables on her feet. Ultimately, she overpowers Aunt Elizabeth, strips her, and escapes in the Aunt's khaki uniform.

Offred leaves the Center and joins the robotic cadre of Gilead's Handmaids. After one failed attempt to conceive, she passes into the possession of a second official, Commander Fred, whose previous Handmaid hanged herself from the bedroom light fixture. Daily, Offred carries a basket to local markets to obtain fresh food, then returns to a boring incarceration in a cloistered room, relieved only by public prayer sessions, birthings, monthly medical exams, and executions. Once a month she mates with Commander Fred in a pseudo-religious ritual requiring Bible reading, followed by copulation with the Commander in the presence of his aging Wife, Serena Joy. A spiteful, unhappy former gospel singer, Serena at first disdains Offred, then grows so despondent at their mutual barrenness that she arranges for Offred to conduct a secret sexual liaison with Nick, the family chauffeur.

Unknown to Serena, the Commander has been summoning Offred to late-night visits to his den for companionship, games of Scrabble, kisses, and gifts of hand lotion, fashion magazines, and information about the outside world. Offred divulges a Latin phrase which her predecessor scratched on the wall. The Commander translates it for her. On one of her visits, the Commander presents her with borrowed finery—makeup, high heels, a sequined and feathered costume, and an evening cloak. Offred abandons her standard red outfit and, dressed in whorish frippery, accompanies him to Jezebel's, an illegal nightclub staffed by prostitutes and frequented by Gilead officials and Japanese and Arab businessmen. Offred locates Moira among the prostitutes and pumps her for information. Moira relates her failed attempt to escape Gilead and reports seeing a documentary film that contained a glimpse of Offred's mother, now an Unwoman at a radioactive Colony.

On a late summer day, Serena confronts Offred with the garish sequined garment and accuses her of treachery. As Offred contemplates her alternatives—escape, suicide, retreat to Nick's quarters, a plea for mercy from the Commander—a black police van arrives. Nick enters her room and hurries her into the custody of two operatives of the Eyes, whom he indicates are double agents for Mayday, the underground liberation group that Ofglen has hinted at. Against the Commander's objections, the two agents charge Offred with violating state secrets and hustle her into the waiting van. Her narrative ends with her ambiguous departure from the Commander's custody.

On June 25, 2195, over two centuries after the formation of Gilead's theocratic dictatorship, an academic consortium listens to a keynote speech delivered by Professor James Darcy Pieixoto, an archivist who gives evidence of Offred's experiences as narrated on thirty cassette tapes. The unnumbered segments do not establish the existence of a real historical figure, but shreds of data suggest that the voice on the tapes belongs to a single speaker who identifies a real Commander, possibly Frederick R. Waterford, who was eradicated during a state purge of liberals. Pieixoto's surmise is that Offred escaped Gilead on the Underground Femaleroad, connected with a Quaker way station in Bangor, Maine, and concealed her story on pre-recorded commercial tapes before departing to either Canada or England. Pieixoto assumes that Offred lived out her life in seclusion to spare her family from lethal reprisals.

CRITICAL COMMENTARIES

EPIGRAPHS

To set the tone of *The Handmaid's Tale*, Atwood opens with three disparate epigraphs, or introductory quotations.

• The first, from Genesis 30:1-3, cites the crux of the scriptural love story of Jacob and Rachel. Having promised to work seven years in exchange for marriage to his uncle Laban's daughter Rachel, Jacob is tricked into marrying the elder daughter, Leah, who bears him two sons. In her jealousy and self-abasement, Rachel, Jacob's second and most beloved wife, insists that he bed her handmaid, Bilhah, who also bears two sons. This biblical event forms the justification for twentieth-century Gilead's Handmaid system as well as a prophecy: women who fail to conceive are devalued.

• The second epigraph comes near the end of "A Modest Proposal," Jonathan Swift's caustically **satiric essay**, published in 1729. Swift's incredibly objective speaker proposes the raising of children for sale as a food and commodity item in order to alleviate the poverty of poor families who produce more infants than they can afford to rear. The controlled, sincere tone of the unnamed proposer of this mad scheme parallels the earnest fanaticism of Atwood's Gilead.

• The final epigraph, taken from an Islamic **proverb**, suggests that there need be no laws against the obvious. Because people were not meant to eat stones, a traveler in the desert would not expect to see a prohibition against such a meal.

Commentary

Atwood conjoins the three epigraphs by drawing on a **controlling metaphor**: the **images** of produce, food, and eating, which create a motif of fulfillment. In Genesis 30, Jacob asks Rachel whether he is to be accused of denying her "the fruit of his womb." Swift's proposal, a cannibalistic economy based on the consumption of young children, supplants "vain, idle, visionary thoughts" in a lame attempt to alleviate social dysfunction. The final epigraph notes that no one seriously considers eating stones. The farfetched **juxtaposition** of these three citations prefigures the extent of the **fantasy** in which prestige and/or survival for enslaved women resides in a waning society's obsession with producing a healthy crop of children for its upper echelon.

To assure proper nourishment in potential mothers, the control of food and the denial of cigarettes and alcohol are crucial factors. Thus, during a war-torn era marked by food shortages and rationing, Offred, like a fatted calf, journeys daily to dairy, meat, grain, and produce markets to buy nourishing milk, bread, chicken, strawberries, and radishes; as the family's hope of viable offspring, she lives literally off the fat of the land. On the down side, Offred's habitation resembles a stall in that she is allowed rest and exercise, but has no freedom of movement to divert her from her task of conceiving. Also, like a brood animal, she must produce within a prescribed time limit or be dispatched to toxic clean-up crews in the Colonies or to Jezebel's, a businessmen's brothel.

(Here and in the following sections, difficult words and phrases are translated for you, as are those below.)

• **Sufi**   a seventh- and eighth-century mystical Arabic sect growing out of Islam. Infused with lyricism and wisdom, Sufism encouraged the faithful to seek God out of love rather than from any desire to gain heaven or avoid hell.

I NIGHT

Chapter 1, the lone segment of Section I, introduces a gymnasium scene in which Alma, Janine, Dolores, Moira, June, and other Handmaids-in-training sleep in a barracks arrangement beneath flannel sheets and army blankets and contemplate their yearnings for freedom. Like girls at a restrictive camp, they reach out to their sisters to learn their names and to touch hands. The women, doubly protected by Aunts, armed with electric cattle prods and whistles, and Angels, or guards, outside the building, receive a brief privilege—twice-daily walks in pairs on an adjacent football field. The inmates fantasize about making deals with the guards, employing sex as a bartering medium.

Commentary

This spare introduction sets up powerful **motifs** that permeate the novel. Floating through the grim, Byzantine setting are after-images of the past, when teams played basketball on the court. Gilead's hierarchy, for all its repression of the past, fails to eradicate normal human activities of the pre-war period. Atwood infuses the scene with sights and smells and sexuality of teenagers of the past era by emphasizing **sense** imagery. Harking further into the past to medieval times, when women were immured in convents, the reference to palimpsest recalls the copyists' method of erasing old manuscripts and refilling them with inscriptions. The method failed to delete the original text, which cropped up in words and letters that recalled fragments of a former message.

A second significant motif is the juxtaposition of innocence and brutality. A cadre of female supervisors bearing the comforting title of "Aunt" patrols like sadistic Amazons. Sleeping inmates lie under fuzzy flannelette and military blankets, a blend of images suggesting the dystopian fusion of gentleness with militarism. The illusion of protection, symbolized by barbed wire atop the chain-link fence, leaves the unsettling question of the inmates' status: are they being nurtured or imprisoned? Their names imply an answer—Alma, which is Latin for *nurturing*, or *kindly;* Delores, which comes from the Latin word for *grief*; and June, reflecting the Roman Juno, goddess of marriage and the family. Likewise, Janine and Moira are romantic versions of John and Mary, two names so enduring that they conjure images of stability and normalcy. Likewise, the aunts, Sara and Elizabeth, bear Old Testament names reflecting motherhood—Sarah, Hebrew for *princess*, the elderly woman who became the mother of the Hebrew nation; and Elizabeth, the aged parent of John the Baptist, forerunner of Christ.

Geometric absolutes, a third motif introduced in these opening paragraphs, prefigure Aunt Lydia's insistence on an either/or philosophy through which she guides future Handmaids in making prudent choices in matters of behavior, morality, and subservience to the state. Like the stripes and circles that outline the basketball court, the rules that govern Gilead create an inflexible, authoritarian environment in which punishment for infractions is swift and arbitrary. In later scenes, Offred contemplates the circle on the ceiling over her bed, where a chandelier once provided light. After her predecessor's suicide, the family removed the light fixture, leaving only an empty, but meaning-packed circle.

- **Aunts** staff members who blend the prim role of academy schoolmarms with the sadism of prison matrons.

- **Angels** a euphemism for soldiers, or guards.

II SHOPPING

In spring, settled in a sedate, suicide-proof chamber, Offred, who is conditioned to accept her lot as a Handmaid as though it were a commission in the army, endures a prissy, overly feminized environment run by women. Her red habit, matched with stockings and gloves and topped with white blinders, isolates her from society as she shops daily for groceries. She sets her goals at unattainable levels—not to think too much so that she can survive repression. Although she longs for feminine companionship and conversation, Offred tries to avoid Serena Joy, the Commander's testy, envious Wife. Undercurrents of murder, assault, and stillbirth float by in the gossip of Marthas, females who guard the household.

To Serena Joy, who has passed her reproductive years, Offred is both "reproach" and "necessity." Five weeks previous to the opening scene, Offred arrived by staff car at the Commander's front door, which Serena blocked in a frail show of domestic dominance. On admittance to the family sitting room, Offred perched on a stiff chair as Serena, cold and nervous, stubbed out black-market cigarettes while outlining house rules: "I want to see as little of you as possible." To Offred, the arrangement was a "business transaction."

On her walk toward the rendezvous with the obligatory second Handmaid, Offred passes Nick, the Commander's cocky chauffeur, who polishes the family Whirlwind; he winks provocatively at Offred. Her reaction is a blend of annoyance and caution. She could report him for insolence, but she fears that he is an Eye, or police spy. At the corner, Offred joins Ofglen, a pious, pro-army disciple of Gileadism who, two weeks earlier, replaced a Handmaid who disappeared inexplicably. Checkpoint guards authenticate street passes by punching in identification numbers on Compuchek. A youthful guard peers at Offred's hidden features and blushes.

The town, so over-regulated and devoid of humanity that it looks like a miniature city, lacks crime, sidewalk litter, and a semblance of normal human habitation. The austere landscape sets Offred on a memory tour of the past, when she shopped with her earnings and wore nail polish and her own clothes. Waiting in line for service at the local market, she observes the stir that accompanies the arrival of Janine, a vain Handmaid who is "vastly pregnant." Again on the streets, Offred walks with Ofglen past the church and the Wall, where six bodies of former abortionists hang like war criminals, reminders of that morning's Men's Salvaging ceremony.

Commentary

Divided into five brief chapters, this segment relates the controlling theme of Atwood's novel: the sterility and coercion of a circumscribed and enforced notion of womanhood. Because Offred's mind longs for stimulation, she wards off the boredom of incarceration by playing word games, twisting "Waste not want not" into an exercise in logic: "If I am not being wasted, why do I want?" In an **existential** brain stretcher, she declares, "I am alive, I live, I breathe, I put my hand out, unfolded, into the sunlight," yet the warm rays fail to penetrate to the chilled soul that doubts the future and longs for news of mother, husband, and daughter. Displaying a sliver of defiance against the dictatorship that has robbed her of family and freedoms, Offred refuses to think of her cell as "my."

The persistent color motif suggesting menstruation and the female cycle resounds in the blatant scarlet color of the Handmaid's uniform, Serena's voluptuous tulips, and the blood spots on the hoods of executed doctors. To Offred, the blood color "defines us." Curiously, Offred's name suggests both "of Fred" and "off red," a hint of her rebellion against authoritarianism. Like a venturesome Little Red Riding Hood in a forest of preying beasts, she steps out of the Commander's protective walls into the streets, her only armament a shopping basket. The **ambiguity** of Offred's position in Gilead is reflected in society's unresolved conflict of interests. As a treasured future mother, she enjoys a bland, but nutritious diet and the constant vigilance of guards, who protect her sexual integrity at the same time they prevent her from taking a subway into the city. As a potential failure, she lives under a sword of Damocles, an unnamed punishment that will fall on her after three years of failed attempts to conceive. Thus, the Handmaid journeys an ambiguous walkway, both "path through the forest" and "carpet for royalty."

- **Waste not want not**   a puritanic aphorism credited to John Platt, nineteenth-century author of *Economy*, a compendium of platitudes.

- **ladies in reduced circumstances**   a Victorian euphemism for poor women, who frequently had to live in boarding houses when they could find no suitable employment. Many of them ultimately resorted to prostitution, turning their rented chambers into brothels.

- **Late Victorian**   an architecture that reflects the staid, family-centered mindset of Queen Victoria's reign, which extended from 1837–1901. A heavy style, the Victorian touch runs to red brick, imposing, fortress-like facades, and an absence of beauty for its own sake.

- **fanlight**   a half-circle of colored glass meant to add filtered overhead sunlight as a further adornment of the foyer. The colors, red and blue, suggest patriotic bunting as well as the free-floating hostility between the Commander's Wife in blue and the intrusive Handmaid in red.

- **pier glass**   a bulging, round mirror that produces a distorted image. Symbolically, it represents the Commander's importance to Gilead's spying operation and the prying eyes that deprive Offred of privacy. In its fish-eye reflection, Offred sees herself as a "sister, dipped in blood."

- **Martha**   In Luke 10:38–42, Martha, a Bethany housekeeper, works so hard at welcoming Jesus to her home that she fails to take advantage of his teachings.

- **scriptural precedent**   biblical examples taken from context and used as justification for Gilead's laws, or strictures. One precedent allows Wives to hit Handmaids.

- **Whirlwind**   a high-powered car that suggests the biblical injunction from Hosea 8:7, a mournful complaint warning wayward Israelites: "They have sown the wind, and they shall reap the whirlwind: it hath no stalk: the bud shall yield no meal: if so be its yield, the strangers shall swallow it up."

- **Compuchek**   a parody of computerized scanning devices that read credit cards and bar-coded pricing and inventory symbols.

- **Commanders of the Faithful**   a euphemism for the privileged, authoritarian hierarchy of Gilead.

- **Salvagings**   a euphemism for executions. Such manipulations of language conceal the predatory nature of Gilead and its vicious hierarchy.

- **Prayvaganzas**   a public display of sanctimony, which occurs in Chapter 33.

- **Birthmobile**   a vehicle that transports Handmaids to a birthing so that they may encourage their fellow Handmaid during labor and profit from the experience by conceiving and producing children for Gilead.

- **Gilead**   in Old Testaments times, a productive Israelite upland region east of the Jordan River and northeast of the Dead Sea. Gilead was known for ample flocks of sheep and goats, orchards and vineyards, and plentiful spices.

- **Econowives**   a jargon term for working-class women who lack maid service and thus must "do everything."

- **Lilies of the Field**   a clothing store that takes its name from the Sermon on the Mount, Matthew 6:28.

- **Milk and Honey**   a food shop named for a biblical allusion to abundance, which is repeated in Exodus 3:8, Exodus 33:3, and Jeremiah 11:5.

- **Libertheos**   a political force that captured Central America and cut off supplies of oranges to Gilead. The name elides the Latin for *free* with the Greek for *god*.

- **Red Center**   an acronym of the official name of Gilead's indoctrination center, the Rachel and Leah Re-Education Center, where potential breeders dress in red habits.

- **All Flesh** Gilead's meat center, taking its name from a warning in Isaiah 40:6 that, unlike God's word, human life is fragile and transitory.

- **women in long somber dresses** the pictures on the walls of the museum depict the area's Puritan ancestry.

- **memento mori** Latin for "remember that you must die," an inscription used by the pious on tombstones and monuments.

III NIGHT

Escaping her chaste confinement through word gymnastics and mental excursions, Offred recalls a college dormitory scene, depicting her friendship with Moira. She also remembers a childhood Saturday in a park, where Offred's mother joined a militant feminist gathering organized to burn pornographic magazines. The scene then shifts to Offred's failed attempt to escape to Canada. She recalls being taken into custody and drugged into oblivion, meant to make her forget the abduction of her daughter. Clinging to sanity, Offred tells her story to an invisible audience, even though she knows that no one can hear her desperate narrative.

Commentary

This brief survey of Offred's suppressed emotional state reminds the reader that a period of violence separates her old life as wife and mother from coercive Handmaid's training at the Red Center and subsequent placement with the Commander's family. Atwood composes loose shreds of **mental scenarios** to ally the three females whom Offred values and remembers in an effort to hold onto hope: Moira, her college friend, and Offred's strong-willed mother and innocent daughter. The grim photo of the child attests to the fact that little girls, who are invaluable to Gilead in a time of widespread infertility and birth defects, may have been shanghaied into another form of fundamentalist manipulation, as suggested by the child's long white dress, the costume worn by Gilead's virginal Daughters. Offred, awakening to a faceless staff, assumes that she has lost track of time while under the influence of sedatives.

IV WAITING ROOM

In May, Offred again joins Ofglen to walk by the Wall; they turn away from an executed trio—a priest and two homosexuals. As three Econowives pass by in mourning for a stillborn fetus, Offred and Ofglen place hands over their hearts in a gesture of sympathy. The Handmaids walk on and part with a sanctimonious ritual farewell, "Under His Eye." Offred sees her own hesitation and fear reflected in Ofglen's tentative move toward communication.

Passing Nick and Serena, Offred returns to the kitchen and delivers the day's supply of groceries to Rita. After Offred climbs the stairs, she passes the Commander outside her room. Alone again, she retreats into enforced seclusion and thinks about her premarital affair with Luke. Suffering an "[attack] of the past," she recalls her arrival at the Commander's house and her investigation of the sparse leavings of the former Handmaid. On her third day, she found scratched into the corner of the closet a bit of Latin doggerel, which she is unable to translate. Her questions to Rita fail to gain information about former Handmaids.

Summer brings lighter garments. Offred is escorted to the doctor's office in a modern office building for her monthly medical examination. After vaginal and rectal probing and breast exam, the doctor whispers through the cloth screen, "I could help you." Offred considers taking a chance on insemination by the doctor, but fears the death penalty. Later, in her bath, Offred avoids gazing on her body because it "determines [her] so completely." Her memories return to a time when a demented woman briefly stole Offred's eleven-month-old daughter from a shopping cart.

On the afternoon of the monthly ritual mating with the Commander, Cora supervises Offred's bath. Offred dresses and dons a red veil in anticipation of the ceremony.

Commentary

This grouping of five chapters delineates more thoroughly the **characterization** and **focus** of Offred. In former times, her life was full of love, friendship, learning, opportunity, and optimism. Although her mother was an actively militant feminist, Offred, a postfeminist backslider, failed to appreciate women's rights and privileges, such as making choices, having a job, holding a bank account, controlling her reproductive capabilities, and enjoying equality with men. She paid scant attention to the ominous political, religious, and social climate that indicated an alarming rise in misogyny. By cocooning herself in Luke, her daughter, and the events of their narrow microcosm, she ignored the gathering hostile takeover until she and her family were victims of Gilead's lethal tentacles.

Under rigorous theocratic rule, seemingly pampered with her diet of chicken, vegetables, fruit, and milk, Offred retains the womanly urge to hide in her spare pair of shoes some pats of butter which she uses as body cream. This small indulgence lightens the tedium of incarceration, as does her reading of "Faith" on the needlepoint pillow and her tolerance of Nick's flirtations. Although willing to flout rules against makeup, reading, and infidelity in these minuscule misdemeanors, Offred is too intent on survival to risk so daring a departure from law as copulating with the doctor, a capital crime for both of the fornicators if they are discovered.

As she examines the tattooed pass number and symbolic eye on her ankle, Offred, like the women of World War II whose heads were shaved for consorting with the enemy, appears to live vicariously on the edge—never far out of compliance, yet a bit of a daredevil. Thus, against a brutally intrusive, all-knowing regime, she retains a frail modicum of individuality and self-esteem. In anticipation of another mating with the Commander, she composes herself into a soulless, long-suffering receptacle for his sperm.

- **sect wars**   interdenominational battles, which Gilead's fundamentalists fight against Jews, Jehovah's Witnesses, Quakers, and other religious sects.

- **gender treachery**   betrayal of traditional sex roles—that is, homosexual acts.

- **All flesh is grass**   a biblical warning in Isaiah 40:6–8, noting that "all the goodness thereof is as the flower of the field. . . . The grass withereth, the flower fadeth; but the word of our God shall stand for ever."

- **Forgive them, for they know not what they do**   Aunt Lydia's pious platitude, drawn from Luke 23:34, repeats one of Jesus's final utterances during his crucifixion at Calvary.

- *Nolite te bastardes carborundorum*   a botched version of the Latin aphorism *Non illegitimi carborundum,* meaning "Don't let the bastards wear you down."

- **Amazing grace . . .**   a popular Protestant hymn written by reformed slaver John Newton, who established a new life as minister and hymn writer.

- **I feel so lonely, baby . . .**   concluding lines from Elvis Presley's "Heartbreak Hotel."

- **Compudoc**   medical computer like the Compuchek, which ascertains patient identity.

- **snake-twined sword**   a version of the caduceus, the traditional symbol of the medical profession.

- **St. Paul**   a founder of Christian worship and writer of epistles to new churches. Paul was notoriously hard on women, particularly the whores of coastal Mediterranean towns, whom he forced to cover their hair as evidence of their departure from seducing sailors and of their conversion to Christianity.

- **that film, about the women**   Offred recalls an unnamed movie picturing female collaborators kneeling in the town square and having their heads shaved in token of their disloyalty.

V NAP

In a single chapter, Offred's tenuous, tedious existence is **summarized** as she waits for the ceremony. She recalls how Handmaid's training prepared her for periods of nothingness and wonders if she were drugged or merely overwhelmed by the enormity of the change in her life. While she practices labor exercises on the floor, her mind drifts back to the Red Center gymnasium and her friendship with Moira. Three weeks after beginning indoctrination, Offred reunited with Moira, who was brought in with a bruise on her cheek. After a four-day wait, the pair managed to slip past a guardian Aunt for a pleasant, but brief afternoon rendezvous in the end stall of the washroom.

After Offred stretches out on the braided rug, amorphous dreams of the past haunt her rest. She remembers standing at the closet in her first apartment, searching her wardrobe for an appropriate dress. Behind her, Luke recedes into the background as the cat demands food. The disjointed **stream-of-consciousness** daydream shifts to her family's abortive attempt to cross the Canadian border. During a chase through the woods, Offred tries to rescue herself and her daughter from faceless pursuers. Shots crack like the snap of dry branches. Hostile forces separate her from the child, who is taken away. In an abrupt shift to the present, the maid rings the bell and awakens Offred to tears and a realization that the loss of her child is her worst dream.

Commentary

Atwood makes extensive use of the isolated chapters that depict Offred coping with loneliness. Bored with unfilled time, Offred battles ennui by pondering paintings of luxuriant, fleshy women in harem settings. Ironically, she sees herself as a kept woman, a **prototype** of "sedentary flesh." Like a "prize pig," she identifies with the groomed show animal or with a pigeon conditioned as part of a psychological experiment. She regrets having no toy similar to the pigs' plaything to amuse her during the long waits between performances.

As Offred studies the change in her attitude toward femininity, the author, speaking clearly through her heroine, enlarges on a central **theme**, the focus of woman as womb, woman as begetter. The round of lunar cycles depresses Offred as her unproductive, pear-shaped uterus becomes a pulsating **symbol**—a pseudo-heart, the glowing core of her existence. The arrival of her menstrual period, "the droolings of the flesh," reduces her to normal fits of the blues, exacerbated by emptiness, grief, and despair, "coming towards me like famine." Taking a secondary role in her body, her beating heart, "salty and red" with its blend of tears and blood, marks the rhythm of days as she awaits conception and the resulting release from a potential death sentence if she fails to produce a child.

By the end of the chapter, the salty blood is supplanted by real tears, which Offred wipes away with her sleeve. The total effect captures the **crux** of the story—the fact that Gilead has performed a dire organ swap, hearts for uteruses. Too fearful of allowing herself to grieve for members of her family who might still be alive, Offred does what prisoners of war do to keep sane. She concentrates on self-control and compliance with her keeper's wishes and wills her reproductive organs to fill the empty chamber with a fetus.

- *Les Sylphides*   a popular ballet adapted in 1909 from music by Chopin and featuring a serene, plotless idyll of graceful, birdlike female beings and a single male dancer.

- **Testifying**   a Gileadean perversion of a fundamentalist ritual in which Christians tell how and why they gave up sinful ways and converted to Christianity. In the futuristic testimony, Handmaids-in-training confess to sexual sins, including gang rape and abortion.

VI HOUSEHOLD

At the bell's summons, Offred descends to the sitting room and kneels. Cora, Rita, Nick, and Serena arrive, waiting for the Commander, who will complete the "household." As in earlier scenes, Offred disengages her mind and returns to a crucial flashback of her family's attempt to escape oppression. By faking visas, packing a picnic, and drugging their daughter, they emulate nonchalance and drive expectantly toward the Canadian border. Offred's flashback memories are interrupted by the Commander's abrupt entry into the parlor, a violation of house protocol.

Exerting a privilege of the man of the house, the Commander unlocks a box and withdraws a Bible, which is off-limits to females. The women stare at him as he calls for a drink of water and dons reading glasses. As he indifferently reads passages from Genesis, Offred recalls reading from the Beatitudes at the Red Center and Moira's failed attempt to feign illness. Offred remembers how Moira was hauled out to the Science Lab and beaten on the soles of her feet, a devious form of torture, leaving no readily visual evidence, administered with frayed steel cables by the darkly menacing Angels. The Handmaids could do little for her except make small gestures of complicity—steal packets of sugar from the cafeteria and pass them to her during the night.

Chapter 16 details the mating ceremony, the central event in Gilead's struggle to survive nuclear havoc. The ritual takes place in a genteel canopied bed. As Offred, robed and veiled, lies between Serena's outspread thighs and clutches her hands, the Commander, also in uniform, mounts Offred and ejaculates. Serena then coldly dispatches the Handmaid from the scene. Offred returns to her room, a setting medieval and nunlike in its innocence and purity. She yearns for Luke's embrace, for worth, for the sound of her real name.

Frenziedly repeating "I want," Offred obeys her urges and gets out of bed. In her zigzag longings for an undelineated assuagement of emotional unrest, she sets out to steal something. Once down the stairs and into the darkened sitting room, she hopes for a knife but, instead, pinches off a fading daffodil bloom to leave in her room for the *next* Handmaid to discover. A click signals the approach of another person. Nick slides into view and pulls her to him for a kiss. He passes on a message: the Commander wants to see her in his office the next day.

Commentary

Exuding sexuality, the **prelude** to the mating scene blends details and **images** into a sensual, pre-coital symphony: Nick twice nudges Offred with his foot, flowers become "the genital organs of plants," and a televised male choir punctuates the refrain of "The Little Brown Church in the Vale" with the bass counterpoint, *"Come, come, come, come,"* an obvious reference to ejaculation. Truncated by a switch to televised video clips of religious warfare in Detroit, the news concludes with a benevolent, grandfatherly anchorman—a fictional version of Walter Cronkite—who convinces the audience that All Is Well in Gilead. After the appearance of the Commander, the sexual overlay intensifies with phallic images ("his extra, sensitive thumb, his tentacle, his delicate, stalked slug's eye, which extrudes, expands, winces, and shrivels back into himself") and copulative **metaphors** ("this journey into a darkness while he himself strains blindly forward"). Offred, who is simultaneously amused and compromised by the Commander's power, quips, "I've got my eye on you. One false move and I'm dead," a snippet of **black humor** that captures the potential for tragedy in their unproductive copulation.

The mating scene contains, literally and figuratively, the novel's climax. This central **tableau**, like a religious sacrament from the Middle Ages, exalts Serena as a madonna figure at the same time that it demeans Offred, the Handmaid. Contrasting the red and white of Offred in her upstairs quarters, the subtler apricot-hued, tufted carpet and leather upholstery set against dusky rose velvet curtains provide a fashionably domestic ambience for the room's focus—a cloyingly **cliché** white china Cupid leaning its arm on a lamb and flanked by two pairs of silver candlesticks. The enigma of dried arrangements alongside "real daffodils on the polished marquetry end table" epitomizes the **paradox** that is Serena—wizened, but alive; brittle, yet feminine; hard, but sentimental. Over the visual images floats the sickly-sweet scent of lily of the valley, a fragrance that Offred connects with "the innocence of female flesh."

As living proof of the Latin saying, *Post coitum omne animal triste,* Offred's response to intercourse is an amplified version of post-coital sadness, the after-effects of anticipation and exploitation. In the arms of Nick, her fantasy figure, she exults in the taste of his skin and exonerates her greed for touch and guilt-laden lust by addressing Luke, "It's you here, in another body." Nick's covert message underscores the Handmaid's pawn-like helplessness—the Commander expects her the next day for a private interview. In response to the summons, Offred clutches the door knob and acknowledges her impotence: "It's all I can do."

- **a parlor, the kind with a spider and flies**   an allusion to the nursery rhyme that begins with "Come into my parlor, said the spider to the fly." The parallel between the sticky web and Serena's sitting room echoes the theme of entrapment and powerlessness.

- **Lily of the Valley**   In the Song of Solomon 2:1, the chaste bride refers to herself as "rose of Sharon" and "lily of the valley." This seemingly erotic verse was allowed to remain in the **canon** works of the Bible after interpreters saw a parallel between Christ, the bridegroom, and his beloved, the Church. In gospel lyrics, the genders are reversed so that Christ becomes the "lily of the valley, the bright and morning star, the fairest of ten thousand."

- **"Come to the Church in the Wildwood"**   an enticingly idyllic gospel hymn that depicts worship as bucolic, innocent, and inviting.

- **Angels of the Apocalypse, Baptist guerrillas, Angels of Light** satiric parodies of holy war in which euphemistic names deflect the murderous intent of religious sects fighting for supremacy. The biblical vision of an Apocalypse, when the powers of darkness challenge the powers of light, appears in Revelation 8:2–11:19.

- **national resources**   figuratively, fertile women.

- **Quakers**   a pacifist religious sect that masterminded much of the Underground Railroad and helped escaped slaves elude patrollers as they followed the trail north to New England or Canada.

- **Children of Ham**   a reference to black-skinned nations in Genesis 10:6, a passage that bigoted religious groups use as justification for racism.

- **National Homeland One**   a parallel to schemes by Marcus Garvey and others who sought to resettle African slaves in their native land.

- **"Whispering Hope"**   a familiar gospel hymn suggesting the fleeting hopes of Handmaids who may remain alive only if they conceive.

- **Compucount**   a parody of modern credit cards.

- **Be fruitful, and multiply, and replenish the earth**   the second half of Genesis 9:1, God's injunction to Noah and his family after the ark survived the flooding of the world to rid it of wickedness.

- **Beatitudes**   a reference to the Sermon on the Mount in Matthew 5:3–11, a lyrical passage written in tight **parallelism**. Manipulative propagandists add "Blessed are the silent," which Offred recognizes as a spurious interpolation.

- **"And Leah said, God hath given me my hire, because I have given my maiden to my husband"**   Leah's comment at the birth of Issachar, Jacob's fifth son, Genesis 30:18.

- *papier poudre*   a sheaf of thin paper sheets permeated with face powder. At the turn of the century, these matchbook-sized leaves of make-do cosmetics fit easily into a purse for a quick, surreptitious repair of a shiny nose or face.

- **"For the eyes of the Lord run to and fro throughout the whole earth, to know himself strong in the behalf of them whose heart is perfect towards him"**   II Chronicles 16:9, an analysis of military victory, which occurs through human dependence on God. The passage, as interpreted by Gilead's cabal, justifies the use of the Eyes to spy on citizens.

- **"The moon on the breast of the new-fallen snow"**   an evocative line from Clement Moore's *A Visit from St. Nicholas* (1823). Offred's recitation of a verse from children's poetry suggests a female breast, purity, her fall from innocence, vulnerability, and the cycles of the moon, symbolic of fertility.

VII NIGHT

The urgent need for human contact forces Offred into the past, when she and Luke lay in bed as their unborn child kicked in her mother's womb. Three unsubstantiated visions of Luke flash onto Offred's mental screen:

- Luke lying in underbrush, his soft tissue decayed, leaving a skeleton and evidence of bullet holes through the skull. Offred prays that at least one shot ended Luke's agony in a single, brief spasm.
- Luke captured and held in prison, his hair and beard ragged, his appearance ten years older than she remembers him. His rights denied, he remains imprisoned without formal arraignment and refuses to tell his captors what they want to know.
- Luke swimming across the river into Canada and welcomed by Quakers, who dress him warmly. They smuggle him from house to house until he reaches the U.S. government-in-exile.

Commentary

The motif of rescue is a common thread in books by and about women—for example, *Jane Eyre, Gone with the Wind, Farewell to Manzanar, Beloved,* and *The Kitchen God's Wife.* Atwood, who is too determined, too realistic a feminist to accord all the credit to male characters, follows Charlotte Brontë, Margaret Mitchell, Jeanne Wakatsuki Houston, Toni Morrison, and Amy Tan in emphasizing the main character's reliance on self rather than on a fantasized savior—that is, Superman swooping down to save Lois Lane or Dudley Do-Right rescuing the hapless Nell. For Offred, the way out comes from within. While she chafes at her powerlessness and remains candid about her chances of survival, she allows her mind to fondle and caress memories of Luke, but concerns herself with the loss of love rather than with the absence of a protector.

Analyzing the torpor that immobilizes the spirit of Gilead, Offred concludes, "Nobody dies from lack of sex. It's lack of love we die from." Her mental anguish repeatedly frames her imagined pictures of Luke. She toys with her beliefs—that Luke died instantly; that he survives in prison and can feel her thoughts, which she transmits telepathically; that he will some day get a message to her, urging her to be patient and that he will one day reunite their family. In a simulation of the Christian Trinity—Father, Son, and Holy Ghost—the three-in-one vision of Luke impels Offred to "believe in all of them, all three versions of Luke." Her ambivalence torments her in shifting contradictions: "This also is a belief of mine. This also may be untrue." Her mind fastens on standard Puritan gravestone symbolism: an anchor and an hourglass and the words *In Hope.* Offred ponders who did the hoping, the survivors or the corpse.

- **candles you would light to pray by**   an image suggesting Catholic worship, during which the devout light prayers and pray for the souls of loved ones, particularly those in Purgatory who have not yet reached Paradise. The metaphor suggests the limbo in which Offred's family exists— cut off from one another, possibly incarcerated, tortured, or dead.

- **In Hope**   the brief phrase suggests several biblical passages, particularly Psalm 16:9, an uplifting statement of trust that God promises joy and deliverance from suffering: "Therefore my heart is glad, and my glory rejoiceth: My flesh also shall rest in hope.

VIII BIRTH DAY

Still immured in shifting phantasms of the familiar and reassuring past, Offred sees herself as a mother with her child and also as a child with her mother. To compose her muddled brain, Offred recites litanies, mental gymnastics that exercise her numbed thinking processes. As she ponders the second of the two eggs that she is served for breakfast, she responds instantly to the arrival of the red Birthmobile, the Handmaids' transportation to the birthing chamber of Ofwarren. By separate conveyance, Wives arrive to attend the Commander's Wife, who lies in a downstairs room while Ofwarren and her attendants occupy the master bedroom.

Offred recalls indoctrination sessions with Aunt Lydia and conflicting memories of Offred's mother, an aggressive feminist who supported abortion rights. The primitive tableau of a birthing scene advances from contractions to transition as the baby descends to the birth canal. At the crucial moment, Ofwarren climbs onto the Birthing Stool, a two-seater that accommodates the Commander's Wife behind her. A girl-baby emerges and is quickly washed and passed to the surrogate mother, who names the child Angela.

Emotionally wrung out and exuding sympathetic milk from her breasts, Offred returns home by van in late afternoon. She reverts to the third-hand story of Moira, the gutsy rebel who dismantled a toilet flushing mechanism and used its metal arm to intimidate Aunt

The Handmaid's Tale Genealogy

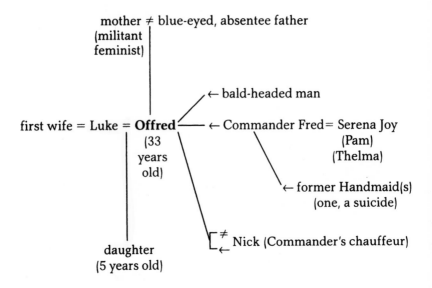

mother ≠ blue-eyed, absentee father
(militant
feminist)

← bald-headed man

first wife = Luke = **Offred** —— ← Commander Fred = Serena Joy
(33   (Pam)
years   (Thelma)
old)

← former Handmaid(s)
(one, a suicide)

daughter   ≠
(5 years old)   ← Nick (Commander's chauffeur)

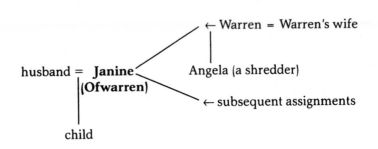

← Warren = Warren's wife

husband = **Janine**   Angela (a shredder)
          (Ofwarren)
                            ← subsequent assignments

child

```
= married to
≠ has sex with
← is mated with
```

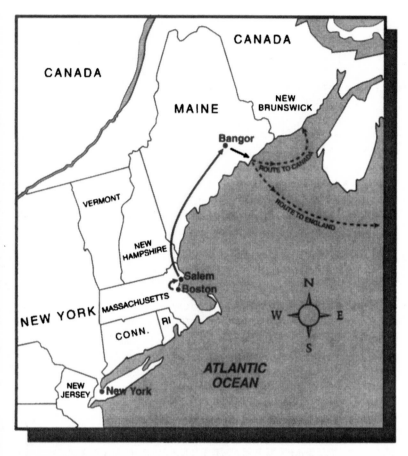

The Femaleroad. Termed "Byzantium in the extreme," Gilead, a fascist republic shaped out of an unnamed New England city by a repressive cabal of the religious right, contains enough texture to suggest a college town reminiscent of Boston. Atwood mentions Massachusetts Avenue, students sculling the river, shoppers riding subways from the outskirts into the heart of the city, and antiquarian interest in old gravestones and colonial architecture. Leaving out secret details, Moira relates to Offred how she escaped Gilead. By connecting with Quaker station tenders of the Underground Femaleroad on a one-to-one basis, Moira reaches the center of the city in a mail sack. Because the border is closely monitored, her route takes her from Salem to a lobster fisherman's home in Maine. She hoped to escape to Canada via the sea route—up the east coast and around the peninsula.

Elizabeth, her hostage. By forcing her victim into the furnace room and exchanging her red clothes for the Aunt's khaki outfit, Moira escaped undetected, leaving Aunt Elizabeth for seven hours before the authorities discovered Moira's escape. While investigating, Aunt Lydia urges Janine, a willing stooge, to stay alert for information from the other inmates.

Keeping Moira before her as a model of courage, Offred intends to escape. She is awakened the next morning by Cora, a barren lover of children who hopes that Angela's birth is a good omen for Offred and the Commander's family. At nine that night, Offred breaks rules and enters the Commander's office and joins him in a game of Scrabble. To her, the illicit tryst is a bargaining session, from which she may obtain some concession. Before she leaves, he requests a sincere kiss.

Commentary

This segment, a complex and interwoven view of womanhood, juxtaposes Gileadean women in variations of power and power-lessness:

- The sadistic, manipulative, khaki-clad Aunt Lydia and her female pupils, whom she vows to "lick . . . into shape," a common idiom that takes on lesbian overtones.
- On the screen of the classroom flickers a training film of an assisted birth, where a woman, "like a broken robot," is contorted and manipulated into giving birth.
- At the home of Ofwarren's family, another paradigm of the female ghetto appears in the social stratification of Wives and Handmaids, a separation of the privileged from the enslaved. Janine, now known as Ofwarren, whimpers "suckily" for a cookie. The indulgent Wife treats her to a sweet, then dismisses her. In private, the Wives snipe, "Little whores, all of them." By the end of the birthing scene, Ofwarren, her temporary prestige cast aside like a discarded afterbirth, retreats into the sisterhood of Handmaids.

Atwood's examination of not only female enslavement but also the complex woman-against-woman undercurrent of innuendo, mistrust, exploitation, and betrayal delves into a dark area of **feminism**—the overlay of treachery that impedes women from trusting their own kind. During this era of repression and coercion, Offred needs spiritual uplift. Out of her dealing with Marthas, Aunt Lydia, Wives, and other Handmaids, the most hopeful relationships come from Moira, who has vanished from Offred's milieu, and Cora, the simple serving woman who manages an occasional smile and perpetual hope for Offred's conception of a child. As an indicator of Cora's consistent, but peripheral encouragement, Atwood has named her for the Latin *cor*, meaning *heart*.

The counterpoint of Gilead's rigid female strata pulsates at different pitches and rhythms—Wives circling the buffet table, sipping wine, gathering in the sitting room. The Wives' mock birthing scene depicts the Commander's Wife in a virginal white gown offset by a spray of gray hair. The coterie of Wives massage her abdomen as though the long-dead reproductive organs were viable, imminently capable of pushing out a living child. In the master bedroom, a similar scene counters with the real push, pant, and relax motif of a woman in the throes of delivery. The local Handmaids, about twenty-five or thirty of them, assist Aunt Elizabeth, the birth master, by running errands and encouraging Ofwarren.

In Offred's mind, another set of female contrasts separates her from her mother, an undaunted voice from the past who lived her life as a liberated woman and took part in public demonstrations for women's rights. During cloaked exchanges at Offred and Luke's residence, Offred's mother referred to Luke as a chauvinist "piglet" and to Offred as a "backlash." Atwood's warning highlights the danger of a **postfeminist** generation of women who take no active interest in women's rights and suffer the consequences when it's too late to stop anti-feminist forces. After the government takeover, Offred—resentful of old arguments with her mother, who expected validation of her philosophies—wishes she could have her mother back again. In a sardonic **invocation** of her mother's spirit, Offred asks, "Can you hear me? You wanted a women's culture. Well, now there is one."

- **paranoid delusion** a perversion of reality. Offred loses touch with identifiable stimuli and fluctuates between testing sanity and denying it. She suspects she is being drugged. To test her grasp of reality, she clutches simple data: " . . . where I am, and who, and what day it is."

- **HOPE and CHARITY** the pillow inscribed with "FAITH" suggests the remaining two abstract nouns of Paul's triad, found in I Corinthians 13:13, "Now abideth faith, hope, charity, these three; but the greatest of these is charity." In Gilead, there is precious little hope or charity; Offred is left with faith in herself.

- **a familiar**   the owl, cat, toad, or other animal that traditionally guards a witch or wizard.

- **an Unbaby**   the one-in-four child born deformed, "with a pinhead or a snout like a dog's or two bodies, or a hole in its heart or no arms, or webbed hands and feet." Atwood's speculative novel suggests that environmental pollution may trigger prenatal malformations, a belief held by agitators against Agent Orange, a defoliant used during the Vietnam War, and the noxious substances said to have affected the reproductive cells of soldiers during the Persian Gulf War.

- **exploding atomic power plants**   an allusion to the nuclear meltdown on Three Mile Island in March 1979. Ironically, Atwood's book was published shortly before the nuclear explosion at Chernobyl, which occurred in Russia on April 26, 1986.

- **San Andreas fault**   a fluctuating fissure in the subterranean plates that threatens the stability of California.

- **Jezebels**   an allusion to the wicked Phoenician, Baal-worshipping wife of Ahab, Israel's king. At her instigation, state-ordered persecution cost the lives of prophets. Her power to subvert the worship of Israel's god with paganism ended in arrest and execution. Her body was devoured by dogs.

- **past the zero line of replacement**   The birthrate has fallen so far that the population no longer grows.

- **carved on the stone walls of caves, or drawn with a mixture of soot and animal fat**   an allusion to prehistoric art, particularly the energetic drawings of Lascaux, a series of isolated chambers in the Pyrenees Mountains between France and Spain, where Neolithic artisans inscribed ritualistic pictures of animals.

- **a handprint on stone**   a reference to the bloody handprints of women who participated in suttee, the sacrifice of Indian wives who followed their husbands' funeral processions, then leaped or were forced onto their crematory pyres. British rulers outlawed the barbaric Hindu custom in 1829, but it continued to thrive in outlying areas.

- **Emerge van**   A shortened version of *emergency*, the Emerge van carries doctors and medical machines to be used only if the "emerge"—the birth—proceeds abnormally.

- **I will greatly multiply thy sorrow . . .**   God's punishment of Eve in Genesis 3:16. The verse concludes with Eve's loss of autonomy: " . . . and thy desire shall be to thy husband, and he shall rule over thee."

- **Agent Orange**   a defoliant employed by the U.S. Army during the Vietnam War to strip the jungle of hiding places for Communist insurgents. Returning soldiers discovered that exposure to the chemical seemingly increased the likelihood of birth defects in their children.

- **Gyn Ed**   education in womanhood, from the Greek *gyne*, meaning *woman*.

- **Birthing Stool**   a primitive seat with a hole in the center. By centering a laboring woman upright on the stool, an ancient midwife utilized gravity to guide the infant out of the birth canal.

- **From each . . . according to her ability; to each according to his needs**   a sexist restatement of a quotation of 1875 from the writings of Karl Marx, father of Communism.

- **Unwoman**   any female remanded to the Colonies to serve in clean-up crews removing toxic wastes.

- **TAKE BACK THE NIGHT**   a feminist slogan of the 1980s indicating dismay and revolt at the increase in violence against women, which lessened their freedoms by making them fear the dark.

- **a circle . . . the stem of a cross**   the traditional scientific symbol for woman. The male counterpart is a circle sprouting an arrow. The two symbols derive from the hand-mirror of Venus and the shield and spear of Zeus. Ironically, the male symbol reflects militaristic strength as opposed to the shallow vanity implied by the female symbol.

- **Aged Primipara**   an elderly first-time mother, as opposed to *multipara*, the medical term for a woman who has borne several children.

- **matrix**   the living tissue in which an embryo grows. The word *matrix* derives from *mater*, the Latin word for *mother*.

- **crowning**   the protrusion from the birth canal of the top of the baby's head.

- **smeared with yoghurt**   that is, smeared with *vernix caseosa*, from the Latin for *cheesy varnish*, the oily protective tissue that coats a newborn.

- **Computalk**   an extension of Compuchek, representative of Gilead's multiple internal forms of electronic communications.

- **black patch**   an advertising ploy for the Hathaway Shirt Company, whose rakish male model often sports a patch over one eye.

IX NIGHT

Offred returns to her room and determines to abandon her reveries of the past and live in the present. Obeying Aunt Lydia's injunction to manipulate men to her advantage, Offred ponders how to bargain for something she needs. Her thoughts turn to women killed in Nazi Germany. As she begins to undress, hysteria grips her emotions. To halt the noise and escape questions and potential extermination by pill or injection, she hides in the cupboard and fingers the scratched message left by her predecessor. Gradually, her breathing returns to normal.

Commentary

Offred's comparisons between the Commander and Hitler are rich with dramatic irony. When rationalizing the camps and the ovens used to rid the Third Reich of anyone whom the Nazis considered unfit citizens, Eva Braun, Hitler's mistress, denied the existence of the machinery of annihilation. She blamed the annihilation of Jews on the exigencies of the times rather than any inherent brutishness in her lover. Her memories of gentle behaviors include his "endearing traits"—for example, whistling off-key in the shower and feeding his dog bits of raw steak. Atwood homes in on a deft barrage of double meanings:

- **showers** the phony hygienic measures that turned out to be outlets for Zyklon-B, a poisonous gas used to kill victims of the SS.
- **truffles** a scarce, edible fungus that is hunted by trained pigs, an evocative image that suggests Hitler's use of the SS to rout out Jews who were in hiding. Implicit in the connection between truffles and pigs is the fact that orthodox Jews refuse to eat pork.
- **Leibchen** a show of affection toward a dog that masks Hitler's monstrous actions toward millions of human victims.
- **raw steak** a symbol of the Third Reich's destruction of victims.
- **melted** a term evocative of the efficient ovens at Auschwitz and other death camps, which filled the skies with the smoke of burning corpses.

- **nightmare** an apt term to summarize Hitler's master plan to rid Germany of undesirables.
- **make-up** a covering of Eva Braun's true feelings about her lover.

- **Context is all** a paraphrase from Shakespeare's *King Lear:* "Ripeness is all" (V, ii, 9). The requests for a game of Scrabble and a kiss, under normal circumstances, would not seem bizarre, but in the context of Gilead, the Commander's desires appear perverted and racy.

- **the man had been cruel and brutal** an allusion to Adolf Hitler, credited with orchestrating the annihilation of over six million Jews, Gypsies, homosexuals, retardates, handicapped, and elderly victims, whom he considered detrimental to the breeding of his Master Race.

- **the mistress** an allusion to Eva Braun, Hitler's mistress, who is thought to have committed suicide with her lover.

- **Liebchen** German diminutive for *darling.*

- **the wandering womb** an ancient Greek explanation for female hysteria, which derives from the Greek *hystera*, or womb

X SOUL SCROLLS

Cora's scream awakens Offred, who pretends that she fainted in the closet. Cora, hoping that fainting is proof of pregnancy, conceals from Rita the fact that breakfast, which Cora dropped on the floor, went uneaten. As a favor to Offred, Cora hides the evidence by flushing the wasted food down the toilet.

In May, Serena appears unaware of Offred's two or three visits per week to the Commander's office. Silently signaled by the off-center placement of Nick's cap, the summons to a night rendezvous draws Offred on tiptoe past Serena's room, where she knits "useless wool people" on an endless series of scarves. Offred plays Scrabble again and receives a gift—a copy of a 1970s *Vogue* magazine. On the third office visit, she asks for hand lotion. He seems surprised that she has no private place to hide valuables.

Copulation rites grow more burdensome when Offred becomes better acquainted with the Commander as she advances from the utilitarian role of concubine to the more titillating status of mistress. She fears that Serena will find out about the night visits and exert the Wife's power over the Handmaid. Outside an automated prayer office, lurking fears cause Offred to guard her questions about God and prayers from Ofglen and to experience relief when secret agents apprehend an unidentified man—anyone except her. Offred continues visiting the Commander and learns that Serena discovered that the Handmaid before Offred was also enjoying secret visits to the den. As Offred gains confidence, she asks the Commander to tell her about the political situation in Gilead.

Commentary

Atwood utilizes nature **imagery** for multiple purposes. The passage of time is obvious by what is in bloom—tulips and daffodils of spring give place to the irises, peonies, pinks, and carnations of May. Serena Joy, kneeling in her garden, snips off seed pods, which, if left on the stem, sap the strength of the next crop of blossoms. Later, the fragrance of overripe flowers signals the end of their season. These **metaphors** of dismemberment, procreative power, and decay reflect the quandary of Offred, who must soon conceive or suffer dire consequences, possibly as an Unwoman in the Colonies. Amid full-plumed willows, spring turf, and bird calls, Offred ponders goddesses and desire and fears for the safety of her melon-like ripeness, which caused a barrier guard a moment's giddiness.

The clandestine evening meetings with the Commander take on a peculiarly sensual **atmosphere**. Like a voyeur, he watches Offred page through a copy of a high-fashion magazine and observes her as she smoothes her hands and face with lotion. These non-sexual intimacies worsen the burden of the Ceremony, which suddenly seems "indecorous, an embarrassing breach of propriety." The Commander, too, loses his objectivity and nearly caresses Offred during their ritual copulation, an unseemly act that could cause her deportation to the Colonies and certain death from radioactive debris. In a moment of ambivalence toward human warmth in a cold, passionless state, Offred acknowledges that becoming the Commander's mistress has advanced her to a status that is more than "a useable body." She concludes, "To him I am not merely empty."

- **fetish** a bizarre or perverse psychological obsession—such as a focus on hair, shoes, revealing lingerie, or body odor—to relieve an erotic need.

- **something Renaissance about the pose**   models depicting bold, self-confident attitudes.

- **We don't seem to have much in common**   a humorous twist on a cliché common to the seductive line of seducers in novels, movies, and television soap operas

- **Colonies**   those areas beyond Gilead that are permeated with radioactive toxins. Clean-up crews consist of incorrigibles, old or sterile women, and other expendable citizens not suited to the rigid caste system of a theocracy or the need for state breeders.

- **Loaves and Fishes**   a food store named for Christ's miracle described in Matthew 14:17 of expanding five loaves and two fish to feed a multitude of hungry people.

- **Daily Bread**   a reference to a line from the Lord's Prayer, found in Matthew 6–11.

- **Women's Salvagings**   a public execution presided over and carried out by women, which is acted out in Chapter 14.

- **Romanesque**   architecture that emphasizes rounded arches and vaults, piers, and arcades.

- **Soul Scrolls**   an automated print shop that publishes prayers "for health, wealth, a death, a birth, a sin."

- **Holy Rollers**   a derisive term applied to energetic religious groups, primarily Pentecostal, who dance, shout, embrace, testify, and speak gibberish during spiritual ecstasy.

- **Tibetan prayer wheels**   cylinders containing written prayers used by devout Buddhists as an adjunct to worship.

- **Identipasses**   in-town visas; an unconstitutional restriction on personal freedom.

- **Pornomarts**   distributors of pornography.

- **Feels on Wheels vans and Bun-Dle Buggies**   vehicles carrying prostitution to the streets.

- **Compunumber**   a credit registration number, a means by which the religious right controls Gilead's apathetic citizens.

- **an F on it instead of an M**   letters denoting gender of cardholders.

- **Ours is not to reason why**   a paraphrase of a line from Rudyard Kipling's "The Charge of the Light Brigade," a war poem describing the pointless deaths of soldiers dispatched into battle against impossible odds.

- **paranoid**   excessively suspicious or mistrustful.

- **semaphore**   a coded system of flag movements used at sea for ship-to-ship or ship-to-shore communication.

- **Hard Times**   a key novel by Charles Dickens depicting the blatant human exploitation common during England's Industrial Revolution.

- **Pen is Envy**   a pun on "penis envy," a concept of Sigmund Freud to account for negative behavior that women express against men.

- *sum es est, sumus estis sunt*   a lesson in beginning Latin, which translates, "I am, you are, he is, we are, you are, they are."

XI NIGHT

The heavy fragrance of summer flowers rises to Offred's bedroom window, where she takes her accustomed seat and gazes out into the night. In the moonlight, she spots Nick. Her thoughts return to her family's failed escape and Luke's killing of the cat, whose prowling and yowls could have given away the family's escape plans. Offred, realizes that the past is slipping from her memory, and prays into the darkness, her loneliness driving her to thoughts of suicide.

Commentary

In her moral dilemma of sexual longing, Offred lusts for Nick as he does for her. From Shakespeare's *King Lear* (V, ii, 9), she rephrases "Ripeness is all" into "Context is all," a **rationalization** for the physical yearning, which is matched by Nick's mateless desires arising from state mandates that deny men of status lower than Commander the sexual privileges of a Handmaid. More than lust, Offred is driven by loneliness—a desire to telephone someone, to conjure up a reason to go on living.

The **parody** of the Lord's Prayer, which takes place by an empty garden just as Jesus prayed alone in the Garden of Gethsemane, verbalizes Offred's feelings of abandonment and despair. Line by line, she restates the sentiments of this central Christian prayer, used at ceremonies and in private devotion as a balanced expression of Christian needs and hopes. Arising from the metaphors of heaven, hell, daily bread, and forgiveness is the specter of the absent chandelier, the anchor to which Offred's predecessor attached her noose. Conjuring like a litany the recurrent line from a tombstone in Gilead's cemetery, Offred tries to remain *In Hope*, but suffers such isolation that she alters her parody into a sincere cry for spiritual sustenance. The chapter concludes with a plaintive **rhetorical question**: "How can I keep on living?"

- **The Fall** Adam and Eve's loss of innocence after they disobeyed God and tasted of the Tree of Knowledge.

- **All alone by the telephone** an Irving Berlin duet sung by Grace Moore and Oscar Shaw in the 1924 version of *The Music Review.*

XII JEZEBEL'S

Whispering cautiously, Ofglen and Offred make their daily trek past the Wall toward the park. Ofglen divulges that "Mayday" is the password of an underground network. On Offred's return to the Commander's house, Serena asks assistance with a skein of wool and reminds Offred that she must soon conceive. Serena suggests that the Commander is sterile and that Offred should emulate Ofwarren and copulate with a surrogate father. Serena proposes that Offred mate with Nick. Offred, who deduces that Serena is sincerely eager for a child, accepts the proposal as a last-ditch effort to conceive. As payment for her role in the conspiracy, Serena hands Offred a cigarette and promises to try to procure a photo of her daughter.

During Offred's nights with the Commander, he grows bolder about drinking and smoking in front of her. He explains the revolution that produced the misogynist state of Gilead: men enslaved women because they had nothing to work for. His explanation is simplistic and patronizing to a woman of Offred's intelligence: "We thought we could do better. . . . Better never means better for everyone. . . . It always means worse, for some."

At a televised Prayvaganza, Offred and Ofglen pass between guards armed with machine guns and enter a covered courtyard. Above the cordoned-off contingent of Handmaids, higher ranking females file into gallery seats. Ofglen points out Janine, newly paired with another family because baby Angela was a "shredder." The ritual group wedding begins with a Commander leading the group in prayers of thanksgiving as twenty white-clad Daughters in their early teens are pledged to twenty Angels, decorated for service at the front. The Commander justifies this method of distributing women as victory prizes—it is an improvement over the "meat market" atmosphere of the old days, when people met in singles' bars or on blind dates. On the way home from the Prayvaganza, Ofglen divulges that she knows about Offred's night sessions with the Commander.

Offred returns to her room and thinks over a mélange of whirling thoughts: about Luke and the old way of "falling in love," about the Latin inscription in the closet, about former times, when women locked their doors to protect themselves from sexual predators. She weeps, "[oozing] like a sponge." Serena enters with a tray of food and a Polaroid picture of Offred's daughter, who is dressed in the white uniform of a Daughter. The likeness of the child, thriving without a mother, saddens Offred, who feels "erased." She eats her creamed corn and contemplates spoon, fork, but no knife.

During a night with the Commander, Offred finds him already well into his evening drinks. He affectionately presents her with a used, sequined, feathered evening garment, high heels, and makeup. Cloaked and hidden on the floor of his Whirlwind car, she accompanies him through checkpoints to the alley behind a former hotel, now a nightclub called Jezebel's. The Commander slips her a purple wrist tag to indicate that she is a paid escort. They enter a room filled with garishly dressed women in bizarre costumes and excessive makeup. The Commander shows her off to club regulars. Offred grows annoyed with his chauvinism.

Among the varied females is Moira, who signals Offred to meet her in the washroom in five minutes. During two visits, Moira fills in details of her escape from the Red Center to the safe house of a Quaker couple, whose names were among those on an underground press list. Refitted in civilian dress, Moira left the house, which was a station of the Underground Femaleroad, hid in a mail sack, and was driven into Boston and on to Salem, where she transferred to a chicken truck bound for Maine. The Quakers intended to move her across the Canadian border by boat. A contingent of "Eyes" ended the escape before Moira got to the dock.

Following torture, Moira viewed a movie on life in the Colonies, where three types of female drays—infertile Handmaids, elderly women, and incorrigibles—and some male "Gender Traitors" disposed of bodies and cleaned toxic dumps and radiation spills. The dangerous work with lethal substances usually kills these outcasts within three years. After a sterilization operation, Moira was allowed a place at Jezebel's, where she works nights and receives good food, drinks, drugs, and face cream as well as the attentions of other lesbians.

Alone with the Commander in an upstairs room, Offred tarries in the bathroom while remembering her mother's disappearance. Wearied, sad, and nearly inert, Offred stretches out beside her lover, who appears old and shrunken after he removes his clothes. He is disappointed by her lack of enthusiasm for illicit sex that is free of the constraints of their monthly ceremonial copulation, which is due to take place the next night. To improve their lovemaking, he proposes turning out the lights. They must return home by midnight.

Commentary

This segment is rich with death **images**. The unexplained *J* on the cadaver at the Wall leaves Offred in doubt about which group the corpse represents, possibly Jesuits or Jehovah's Witnesses. The **tenor** of this passage depicts the intolerance of religious fanatics, who root out all but those who share their dogma. The connection between this scene and the history of the Jewish Diaspora links Gilead with Hitler's Germany, from which Jews escaped, if possible, or stubbornly hid themselves and evidence of their faith from night raiders. In a parallel situation to religious dissidents, Offred identifies with her predecessor, whom she envisions as safe in death, "protected altogether." Like the doomed Handmaid who hanged herself on the chandelier, Offred feels "buried."

The nightclub scene, a stark contrast to the privations of Gilead, delineates the hypocrisy of the **double standard**. For men, physically appealing women from the "old days" become sex toys and bargaining points in trade relations with Arabs and Japanese. To earn the right to serve men, nightclub regulars must keep trim, dress in absurdly scanty garments and push-up bras, smile, dance, and play dumb. Moira's outfit—a parody of a Playboy bunny— recalls the risqué aura of Playboy Clubs of the 1960s, a carry-over from the era of naughty sex, the titillating fantasy atmosphere that preceded the more open and equalized sexual revolution of the

1970s. To Moira, the Commander's decision to bring Offred to the club is "just another crummy power trip."

- **I tell time by the moon**   that is, by her menstrual periods, which parallel the 28-day lunar cycle.

- **yellow stars**   symbols of Judaism selected by Hitler's forces as required badges to identify Jews.

- **Sons of Jacob**   In Genesis 32:28, after wrestling with God's messenger, Jacob changes his name to Israel, thus establishing his tribe as the Israelites, God's chosen people.

- **torahs, talliths, Magen Davids**   symbols of Judaism—the five books of Moses, prayer shawls, and the superimposed triangles that form the hexagrammatic shield of David, a feature of the flag of Israel.

- *M'aidez*   French for "Help me," which is pronounced in English like "Mayday," a universal radio code indicating extreme distress.

- **Aztec hearts**   The ancient Aztecs worshipped at stone altars, where priests used obsidian knives to cut the hearts from sacrificial human victims.

- **Balm in Gilead**   the concluding question in Jeremiah, chapter 8, in which the prophet mourns Judah's slide into wickedness and depravity.

- **Whore of Babylon**   a slang insult found in Shakespeare's *Henry V* (II, iii, 37) and derived from Jeremiah's concern that God's people had taken up Babylonian excesses of bawdy dress, idol worship, and immoral behavior.

XIII NIGHT

That night, the heat in Offred's room grows oppressive, even with the fan. The searchlights are off. Dressed once more in her obligatory red habit and makeup-free face, she awaits Serena, who arrives at midnight to escort Offred through the kitchen and point the way to Nick's quarters. Inside his door, a spartan scene confronts Offred. The denuded walls and barracks-like atmosphere preface a silent, unromantic coupling. Fantasizing, Offred, starved for sexual contact with a man her own age and a social equal, comes alive with passion.

In reality, Offred is unsure of herself and hurries Nick, who makes a crude joke about a passionless act of artificial insemination.

Their seemingly harmless **banter**—"Abstinence makes the heart grow fonder"—causes Offred to cry for all she has lost, "an echo of an echo." Nick caresses her and leads her to the unadorned bed, where he turns down an army-issue blanket. In retrospect, Offred is shamed by her enjoyment of their perfunctory, clandestine intercourse and suffers guilt for betraying Luke.

Commentary

Repeatedly, Atwood superimposes two crucial themes— paranoia and betrayal. In a newly formed theocracy where women can lose all rights to jobs, property, family, name, and self in one swift coup, it is not surprising that Offred wonders whom to trust and how much. After she loses both her job and her personal bank account, the mutually satisfying husband-wife relationship with Luke that produced a little girl instantly withers. In a matter of days, Offred's forced submission to rigid patriarchy allows Luke to control her money and requires that she depend on him for fulfillment, support, and protection. Her private thoughts turn him into a pseudo-enemy—just another male usurping her personhood.

Life at the Commander's house is no better. On daily walks with Ofwarren, Offred hesitates to tell too much and conceals the deal hatched by Serena Joy—a black-market cigarette and a stolen glance at a Polaroid of Offred's daughter in exchange for an illicit servicing by Nick, whose status as chauffeur offers him only a bit more freedom than that accorded Cora, Rita, and the Marthas. Cautiously, expectantly, Offred ventures into the steamy midsummer night, trusting enough in Serena's desire for an infant to risk execution for adultery. Clasped in Nick's arms, and later, when the memories of their shadowy embraces are all she has left to savor, Offred, who only hours earlier shared a bed with the Commander, ponders her betrayal of Luke. Tragic in her uncertainty, she ponders a difficult rhetorical question: "If I knew for certain he's dead, would that make a difference?"

XIV SALVAGING

Wracked with remorse and guilt for the tale that she must finish, Offred admits returning to Nick on the sly, surreptitiously making love by the glare of a state searchlight. Careless of the danger that she courts, Offred talks freely to Nick about Moira and Ofglen, but never of Luke or the Handmaid who died in her room; nor does she talk of *love*, the bad luck word. On daily walks to market, Offred anticipates immediate conception, her mind long past Ofglen's prattling about stealing papers from the Commander's desk or arranging for an escape through underground connections. Offred, for the first time since the takeover in Gilead, is content. Tentatively, she concludes, "I have made a life for myself."

A tolling bell summons all women to a Salvaging. Offred's old hatred of Red Center indoctrination resurfaces, and she gags at seeing Aunt Lydia preside over the execution of two Handmaids and a Wife for an unspecified crime. The event concludes with an added attraction: the Handmaids encircle a Guardian found guilty of raping two women, one of whom was pregnant and who lost the baby as a result of the rapist's brutality. The accused rapist tries to express innocence, but the Handmaids ignore his protestation and kick, jab, tear, and pummel him to death.

This eruption of beast-like violence affects all participants. Mentally unhinged, Janine clutches a tuft of blond hair and babbles innocuously, "You have a nice day." Offred accuses Ofglen of barbarism; Ofglen counters, "They're watching." Returning to her room, Offred tries to comprehend her own active participation in the savage execution, a monstrous emotional release that leaves her famished.

That afternoon, Offred joins a new Ofglen. Cautiously, Offred tests the new girl for loyalty and seeks to extract information about the former Ofglen's whereabouts and about Mayday. Offred fears that the former Ofglen may betray her to the authorities. In terror of harm to Luke, Moira, mother, or child, Offred knows that she would comply with interrogators, even if they aimed reprisals at her family. As Offred turns to go, the new Ofglen whispers, "She hanged herself. . . She saw the van coming for her."

Safe from potential betrayal, Offred embraces the Red Center's teachings, thus capitulating to the insidious power of indoctrination and terrorism. At the steps of the Commander's house, she confronts a new menace—Serena with cloak and sequined garment in hand. Serena grips her cane as she demands, "How could you be so vulgar?" Calmly entering the house by the kitchen door, Offred, basket in hand, ponders the reason for Serena's anger and wonders if she really loves the Commander.

Commentary

Atwood appears to blend her own **persona** with that of Offred as Offred expresses her regrets for the hesitations, distractions, and rapid-fire articulation of the preceding chapters. Offred's tale, recalling the "fried food" heavy hours of incarceration becomes "a body caught in crossfire or pulled apart by force." Atwood seems to apologize for the fragmentary nature of her fable, and her seeming intrusion as a pseudo-voice in the telling of Gilead's agony is actually an artful method of bringing the story to its end. Like a true friend, Offred regrets "this sad and hungry and sordid, this limping and mutilated story" and hopes to hear the reader's experiences, "if I meet you or if you escape, in the future or in heaven or in prison or underground, some other place."

The poignance of Offred's dehumanization echoes against the solid walls, both social and physical, that shut her out of personhood. To maintain a shred of sanity, she copes with madness through her affair with Nick and clings to a fantasized form of what Martin Buber refers to as the I-Thou relationship. "I believe you're there," she asserts, almost like whistling in the dark. "I believe you into being," she admits. In torment, she confesses having sought sexual intimacy repeatedly as though "there will never be any more, for either of us, with anyone, ever." With no moral precepts to guide her choices, Offred, a basically decent, monogamous woman, functions as best she can in the spiritual wasteland that Gilead epitomizes and blames herself for the fading of Luke's image. In face of senseless barbarity and threat of physical and spiritual annihilation, she chants an existential **mantra**, "I am, I am."

- **I tell, therefore you are** a rephrasing of René Descartes' "I think, therefore I am."

- **The bell is tolling** an allusion to John Donne's *Meditation XVII*, which includes the phrase " . . . therefore never send to know for whom the bell tolls; it tolls for thee."

- **Christmas crèche** a manger scene displaying the Holy Family.

- **Bestow** an ironic usage of a biblical synonym for *give*.

- **Particicution** execution by dismemberment.

- **Deuteronomy 22:23-29** the exacting Mosaic law governing punishment for rape of a virgin.

- **Word perfect** the trademark of a popular computer word processing program.

XV NIGHT

At the window of her room, Offred ponders her disgrace. She weighs her alternatives:

- suffocation by setting the house on fire
- escape via a rope of bedsheets draped out the shatterproof window
- confession to the Commander and a plea for mercy
- hanging by bedsheets in the closet
- a surprise attack on Serena, whose murder would also end Offred's life through the resulting execution
- escape out the door and down the street as far as Offred can flee in her giveaway red habit
- sanctuary in Nick's room

The unforeseen arrival of a black police van deepens Offred's dread. Suddenly, Nick enters her room and urges her to go with agents from Mayday. Clutching at his call for trust, she exits with two unidentified men. On her way through the foyer, she passes Serena and the Commander, who demands a warrant for so abrupt and irregular an intrusion into his home. Offred's escort claims that she has violated state secrets. Serena calls her a bitch; Cora weeps.

Commentary

Unable to assess her situation, Offred faces a **dilemma.** Without Ofglen's ties to Mayday and lacking the sympathy and assistance of Serena, Offred has little choice but to trust that the van that takes her away is truly part of a bogus arrest and that she is entering light rather than darkness. The ambiguity of this final view of Offred leaves many questions:

- Is she being rescued or betrayed?
- What is her destination?
- Is she pregnant with Nick's child?
- Is Nick a member of the Eyes or a double agent for Mayday?

63

- Will Offred be reunited with any of her family, assuming that they are still alive?
- What is her real name?

The reader's immersion at this point in the novel is what Aristo-:le refers to as "the willing suspension of disbelief," a bonding with a fictional character who is so believable that he or she is perceived as real. So palpable are Offred's humanity and need that her disappearance into the van suggests a kind of death, both physical and spiritual. So empty is her store of emotional strength that the reader must confront honest doubts that she survives the wiliness and duplicity of the Eyes of Gilead.

- **Nick, the private Eye**   a pun linking the chauffeur with Nick Charles, sleuth in *The Thin Man*, a popular 1934 movie starring William Powell, with Myrna Loy portraying Nora, his wife and sidekick. Peter Lawford reprised the role in a television series of the same name.

HISTORICAL NOTES ON *THE HANDMAID'S TALE*

On June 25, 2195, approximately two centuries after Gilead's hostile takeover, the Gileadean Studies' Twelfth Symposium meets at the University of Denay, Nunavit. The Chair, Professor Maryann Crescent Moon, indicates in her welcome to delegates that the creation of the Gileadean theocracy caused a remapping of the world. The keynote speaker, Professor Pieixoto, casts doubt on a manuscript pieced together from transcriptions of thirty unnumbered tapes, dubbed by Professor Wade *The Handmaid's Tale*, which were unearthed in an army surplus footlocker at a way station of the Underground Femaleroad in Bangor, Maine.

To answer questions of how, when, and by whom the tapes were made and stored, Pieixoto searched fruitlessly for information about the safe house in Bangor, then resorted to an examination of the few remaining printouts from Gilead, which were smuggled to England by Save the Women societies. He deduces that Offred was "among the first wave of women recruited for reproductive purposes" during a period when birthrates for whites were plummeting from use of birth control as well as from infertility, a virulent strain of syphilis, AIDS, stillbirths, miscarriages, and genetic deformities brought on by nuclear waste, chemical and biological weapons, toxic dumping, pesticides, and other deadly pollutants.

The speaker surmises that Offred, who never reveals her real name, may have concealed other characters' identities with pseudonyms. Data from the diary of Wilfred Limpkin identifies two Freds in early Gilead—Frederick R. Waterford and B. Frederick Judd, both Commanders and directors of the Eyes. The former, the husband of Thelma Waterford, was killed in a purge for liberal leanings and for harboring a turncoat. He seems a possible candidate for Offred's gray-haired Commander. Pieixoto surmises that Offred may have escaped to Canada or England, but chose not to go public with her story out of fear of retaliation against her family. Another possibility is that Offred's emotional sufferings forced her into seclusion.

Commentary

Posed at the end of the novel in the form of an author's **appendix**, this **coda** provides a framework and tongue-in-cheek historical perspective for Gilead's story. Atwood's abrupt shift in tone to witty **repartee** and **punning** benefits the work in several ways:

- Self-important, supercilious academic humor lightens the intense and chilling conclusion to Offred's eerily bland recorded **narrative**.
- **Details** revealed in Professor Pieixoto's speech extend some hope that she found her way to a Bangor way station and had enough time and freedom to locate a tape recorder and narrate her experiences in Gilead.
- Additional facts indicate that the theocratic repression found in Gilead also existed in Seattle, Washington, and Syracuse, New York.
- The method of ordering and communicating historical data in Offred's day authenticates and legitimizes **memoir** and **diary** as indigenous literary outlets of oppressed women.
- The **incongruity** of recycled tapes by Elvis Presley, Boy George, Mantovani, Twisted Sister, and Lithuanian folksingers heightens the comic departure from Offred's dire situation. Also, the **implications** of each musical performance carry their own freight of meaning: Elvis, an idolized superstar and sex symbol; Boy George, a British rock singer who cultivates a bisexual image; Mantovani, a name synonymous

with hypnotically bland elevator music; Twisted Sister, a heavy metal rock group whose name echoes Gilead's perversion of womanhood; and Lithuania, a former free state subsumed by the Soviet Union in 1940.

- The nauseating political correctness of Pieixoto, who hesitates to side with Offred's account of murderous oppression in Gilead.

- **University of Denay, Nunavit** a pun on "Deny none of it." Nunavit suggests Nunivak, a fogbound island off Alaska in the Bering Sea. Likewise, the Déné, who are Native American ancestors of the Athapascan aborigines, inhabit the Northwest Territories of Canada south of the tree line. Another sound-alike is Danae, the character from Greek mythology who was impregnated by a ray of sunlight from Zeus while she was imprisoned. After giving birth, Danae and her child were cast into the sea. The conclusion to her story, like that of Offred, is ambiguous, suggesting both acceptance and treachery.

- **Pieixoto** Pieixoto's name suggests Pope Pius IX, a Vatican pope (1854–1878), who, in his first year of office, issued the doctrine of the Immaculate Conception of the Blessed Virgin Mary. The reign of Pius IX produced a sharp swing from liberalism as the Church fought to maintain its powers from diminishment by the aftermath of Napoleon III's rise to power. As a result of the hostile political climate at a time when Rome became a part of the Italian kingdom, the state vs. church power struggle rendered Pius IX a virtual prisoner in the Vatican.

- **Krishna** a light-hearted, sensual Hindu god connected with music and dance.

- **Kali** a paradoxical Hindu goddess of creativity and destruction.

- **The Warsaw Tactic: Policies of Urban Core Encirclement** In 1940, Nazi occupation forces confined 400,000 Jews to a ghetto in the center of Warsaw, Poland. As disease, starvation, and exportation to death camps decimated the number of Jews, the authorities began reducing the perimeter of the ghetto, thus squeezing the inhabitants into a smaller and more easily controlled compound. On April 19, 1943, German and Lithuanian soldiers joined Polish firemen and police in a brutal attack against the remaining 60,000 Jews, who put up a brave, but doomed resistance. By May 16, a house-by-house search revealed that Warsaw's Jews were annihilated.

- **Sumptuary Laws** legal regulation of food, drink, color and style of clothing, personal adornment and purchase and display or use of luxury items, such as furs, glass windows, chimneys, and dishes made of silver or gold.

- **Monotheocracies**   religious dictatorships based on the worship of one god.

- **Arctic char**   a pun on a small-scaled trout and the British slang for *charwoman*, a domestic worker.

- **soi-disant manuscript**   a French literary term questioning the authenticity of a manuscript.

- **in homage to the great Geoffrey Chaucer**   author of *The Canterbury Tales* (1385), a series of narratives told by a contingent of pilgrims traveling to a religious shrine in Canterbury, England. Each tale is identified by the profession or social status of the teller—that is, the wife of [from] Bath, the knight, the nun's priest, the franklin, and so forth.

- **Bangor, Maine**   city in south central Maine. Brewer, across the bridge from Bangor, was once a Quaker waystation on the Underground Railroad. The town's location on the Penobscot River made it a useful connection point to seagoing vessels. From Brewer, abolitionists could transport escaping slaves downriver to the Atlantic Ocean and northeast around the coast to Canada.

- **Frailroad**   a multiple pun on Women as the weaker sex and the pejorative slang term *frail*, meaning a girl or woman. The term also suggests a line from a scene in William Shakespeare's *Hamlet*, in which the title character disparages his mother, Gertrude, a widow newly married to her husband's brother. In disgust at her haste to remarry, Hamlet mutters: "Frailty, thy name is woman" (I, ii, 146).

- **recollected, if not in tranquility, at least** *post facto*   an allusion to William Wordsworth's *Preface to the Lyrical Ballads*. This deduction suggests that Offred lived long enough "after the fact" to compose her thoughts, when safety, privacy, cassette tape, and recorder were available.

- **serial polygamy**   the practice of marriage, divorce, and remarriage.

- **simultaneous polygamy . . . in the former state of Utah**   The reference is to the Mormon practice of polygamy, a socio-religious custom allowing men to take multiple wives, which thrived under the leadership of Joseph Smith and Brigham Young from 1843 until it was banned in 1890.

- **Eurydice** in Greek mythology, the luckless bride bitten by a snake on her wedding day. Her husband, Orpheus, the famed musician, convinced Hades to let Eurydice return to earth. However, Orpheus disobeyed the strictures of the journey and looked at Eurydice too soon, thus dispatching her back to the abode of the dead forever.

CRITICAL ESSAYS

LITERARY ANALYSIS

A one-of-a-kind tour de force, Margaret Atwood's futuristic *Handmaid's Tale* refuses categorization into a single style, slant, or genre. Rather, it blends a number of approaches and formats in a radical departure from predictable **sci-fi** or **thriller fiction** or feminist literature. Paramount to the novel's success are the following determinants:

- **existential apologia** a defense and celebration of the desperate coping mechanisms by which endangered women survive, outwit, and undermine devaluation, coercion, enslavement, torture, potential death sentences, and outright gynocide. Like Zhukov in Alexander Solzhenitsyn's *One Day in the Life of Ivan Denisovich,* Offred clings to sanity through enjoyment of simple pleasures: smoothing lotion on her dry skin and smoking a cigarette with Moira and her lesbian sisterhood in the washroom at Jezebel's; remembering better times with her mother, husband, and daughter, even the veiled sniping between Luke and his mother-in-law; recollecting the pleasant frivolities and diversions that women once enjoyed—for example, eye makeup, fashions, and jewelry, and women's magazines; and allowing herself moderate hope for some alleviation of present misery, although Offred never gives way to a fantasy of rescue, reunion with her family, and return to her old life.
- **oral history** a frequent vehicle of oppressed people who, by nature of their disenfranchisement through loss of personal freedoms, turn to the personal narrative as a means of preserving meaningful experience, and to recitation of eyewitness accounts of historical events in an effort to clarify

gaps, myths, errors, and misconceptions. Similar to Jane, the participant in the Louisiana civil rights movement and title character in Ernest Gaines' fictional *Autobiography of Miss Jane Pittman*, and to Jack Crabb, the bi-national spokesman and picaresque participant at the Battle of the Little Big Horn in Thomas Berger's *Little Big Man*, Offred offers an inside view of the effects of political change on ordinary citizens— that is, the powerless, who are most likely to suffer from a swift, decisively murderous revolution. As a desperate refugee on the "Underground Frailroad," her harrowing flight contrasts the knowing titters of the International Historical Association studying Gilead from the safety of women's rights and academic freedom two centuries in the future.

- **speculative fiction** a form of jeremiad—an intentionally unsettling blend of surmise and warning based on current political, social, economic, and religious trends. As a modern-day Cassandra, Offred seems emotionally and spiritually compelled to tell her story, if only to relieve the ennui of her once nun-like existence and to touch base with reality. Her bleak fictional narrative connects real events of the 1980s with possible ramifications for a society headed too far into conservatism and a mutated form of World War II fascism. By frequent references and allusions to Hitler's Third Reich and its "final solution" for Jews, Atwood reminds the reader that outrageous grabs for power and rampant megalomania have happened before, complete with tattoos on the limbs of victims, systemized selection and annihilation, virulent regimentation, and engineered reproduction to produce a prevailing Caucasian race.

- **confession** an autobiographical revelation of private life or philosophy intended as a psychological release from guilt and blame through introspection and rationalization. Like the weeping survivors of the doomed boy-kingdom in William Golding's *Lord of the Flies* and Holden Caulfield rehashing his failures and foibles from a private California psychiatric hospital in J.D. Salinger's *Catcher in the Rye*, Offred frequently castigates herself for trying to maintain her humanity and fidelity to cherished morals and beliefs in a milieu that crushes dissent. In frequent night scenes, during which Offred gazes through shatterproof glass into the night sky in an effort to shore up her flagging soul, her debates with herself reflect the thin edge that separates endurance from crazed panic. By the end of her tale, she has undergone so much treachery and loss of belief and trust that the likelihood of total mental, spiritual, and familial reclamation is slim. The most she can hope for is physical escape from the terrors of Gilead and the healing inherent in telling her story to future generations.

- **dystopia** an imaginary world gone sour through idealism that fails to correspond to the expectations, principles, and behaviors of real people. In the face of rampant sexual license, gang rape, pornography, venereal disease, abortion protest, and the undermining of traditional values, the fundamentalists who set up Gilead fully expect to improve human life. However, as the Commander admits, some people are fated to fall short of the template within which the new society is shaped, the ethical yardstick by which behavior is measured. His chauvinistic comment is significant in its designation of "some people." These "some people" are nearly all female, homosexual, underground, and non-fundamentalist victims—a considerable portion of the U.S. population.

Indigenous to dystopian fiction is the perversion of technology, as evidenced in *Brave New World, 1984, Anthem,* and *R.U.R.* In Margaret Atwood's *Handmaid's Tale,* loss of freedom begins with what appears to be merely a banking error. Only after repeated attempts to access her funds does Offred realize that control of assets no longer exists for the women of Gilead. From credit card subversion, the faceless radical hierarchy moves quickly to presidential assassination, murder of members of Congress, prohibition of women from schools and the work force, control of the media, and banning of basic freedoms. Without books or newspapers, telephones or television, Offred has no means of assessing the severity of society's deprivations. Controlled by Identipasses, Compudoc, Computalk, Compucount, and Compuchek, she must rely on the most primitive measures of gaining information and securing hope, even the translation of scrawled Latin doggerel on her closet wall. Interestingly, Atwood does not resort to farfetched wizardry. Her astute use of televangelism, cattle prods, credit cards, roadblocks, border passes, computer printouts, barbed wire, public executions, and color-coded uniforms reflects the possibilities of subversion of current technology and social control devices.

LITERARY DEVICES

Like a portion of modern fiction writers—Ray Bradbury, Fred Chappell, and Toni Morrison—Margaret Atwood is, by nature, training, and profession, a poet. Her facile expression of thought processes and manipulation of language to probe the psychological perversions in Gilead produce fascinating, multi-level **rhetorical** maneuvers, often juxtaposing weakness with power or cruelty with vulnerability. For instance:

Simile
- We would exchange remedies and try to outdo each other in the recital of our physical miseries; gently we would complain, our voices soft and minor key and mournful as pigeons in the eaves troughs.
- His skin is pale and looks unwholesomely tender, like the skin under a scab.

Symbol
- I read about that in Introduction to Psychology; that, and the chapter on caged rats who'd give themselves electric shocks for something to do.
- The camera moves to the sky, where hundreds of balloons rise, trailing their strings: red balloons, with a circle painted on them, a circle with a stem like the stem of an apple, the stem of a cross.

Humor
- There's a wad of cotton attached to the back, I can see it as she half turns; it looks like a sanitary pad that's been popped like a piece of popcorn. I realize that it's supposed to be a tail.
- *Is anything wrong dear?* the old joke went.
  No, why?
  You moved.

Alliteration
- In the curved hallway mirror, I flit past, a red shape at the edge of my own field of vision, a wraith of red smoke.

- As for us, any real illness, anything lingering, weakening, a loss of flesh or appetite, a fall of hair, a failure of the glands, would be terminal.

Historical and Cultural Lore
- Dances would have been held there; the music lingered, a palimpsest of unheard sound, style upon style, an undercurrent of drums, a forlorn wail, garlands made of tissue-paper flowers, cardboard devils, a revolving ball of mirrors, powdering the dancers with a snow of light.
- Behind this sign there are other signs, and the camera notices them briefly: FREEDOM TO CHOOSE. EVERY BABY A WANTED BABY. RECAPTURE OUR BODIES. DO YOU BELIEVE A WOMAN'S PLACE IS ON THE KITCHEN TABLE?

Literary Allusion
- I would not be able to stand it, I know that; Moira was right about me. I'll say anything they like, I'll incriminate anyone. It's true, the first scream, whimper even, and I'll turn to jelly, I'll confess to any crime, I'll end up hanging from a hook on the Wall. [recall Winston's capitulation to Big Brother in George Orwell's *1984*.]
- But the frown isn't personal: it's the red dress she disapproves of, and what it stand for. [Parallel the shunning of Hester Prynne, wearer of the red *A* in Nathaniel Hawthorne's *The Scarlet Letter*.]

Aphorism
- Try to pity them. Forgive them, for they know not what they do.
- They also serve who only stand and wait.

Parody
- My God. Who Art in the Kingdom of Heaven, which is within.
- "Blessed be the fruit," she says to me, the accepted greeting among us.

Parallel Construction
- I want to go to bed, make love, right now. I think the word *relish*. I could eat a horse.

- Fake it. . . . Bestir yourself. Move your flesh around, breathe audibly.

Dialogue
- "I didn't know Ofglen very well," I say. "I mean the former one."

  "Oh?" she says . . .

  "I've known her since May," I say . . . "Around the first of May I think it was. What they used to call May Day."

  "Did they?' she says, light, indifferent, menacing.
- "I could help you," he says. Whispers.

  "What?" I say.

  "Shh," he says. "I could help you. I've helped others."

  "Help me?" I say, my voice as low as his. "How? . . . "

  "How do you think?" he says . . .

Foreshadowing
- She held her own hands out to us, the ancient gesture that was both an offering and an invitation, to come forward, into an embrace, an acceptance. In your hands, she said, looking down at her own hands as if they had given her the idea. But there was nothing in them. They were empty.
- "Mayday," she says. "I tried it on you once."

  "Mayday," I repeat. I remember the day. *M'aidez.*

  "Don't use it unless you have to," says Ofglen.

Biblical Allusion
- *Give me children, or else I die.* There's more than one meaning to it.
- "Resettlement of the Children of Ham is continuing on schedule," says a reassuring pink face, back on screen. "Three thousand have arrived this week in National Homeland One, with another two thousand in transit."

Historical Allusion
- Possibly, we reasoned, this house may have been a "safe house" on the Underground Femaleroad during our period, and our author may have been kept hidden in, for instance, the attic or cellar there for some weeks or months, during which she would have had the opportunity to make the recordings.
- The need for what I may call birth services was already recognized in the pre-Gilead period, where it was being inadequately met

by "artificial insemination," "fertility clinics," and the use of "surrogate mothers," who were hired for the purpose.

Sense Impression
- Down there in the lawn, someone emerges from the spill of darkness under the willow, steps across the light, his long shadow attached sharply to his heels.
- Once we had to watch a woman being slowly cut into pieces, her fingers and breasts snipped off with garden shears, her stomach slit open and her intestines pulled out.

Repetition
- *I am, I am,* I am, still.
- Night falls. Or has fallen. Why is it that night falls, instead of rising, like the dawn?

Euphemism
- Guns were for the guards, specially picked from the Angels.
- "Think of it as being in the army," said Aunt Lydia.

Philosophy
- Even though some of them are no more than fourteen—*Start them soon* is the policy, *there's not a moment to be lost*—still they'll remember.
- Nature demands variety, for men. It stands to reason, it's part of the procreational strategy. It's Nature's plan. . . . Women know that instinctively. Why did they buy so many different clothes, in the old days? To trick the men into thinking they were several different women.

WOMEN IN *THE HANDMAID'S TALE*

Atwood, who is famous for depicting themes of betrayal and treachery through the creation of strong and vulnerable female characters, produces a vivid set of possibilities with the women of *The Handmaid's Tale.* The interplay between Aunts and Handmaids-to-be creates an intense effort at subjugation and indoctrination. The creators of Gilead show foresight in turning woman against woman, a method similar to Hitler's use of prison trustees for some of the more onerous jobs of his death camps, particularly the placement of victims in ovens and burial details for those mowed down by machine gun fire. Although Offred resists brainwashing, her regular references to Aunt Lydia's tedious, one-dimensional precepts and aphorisms ["Modesty is invisibility"] indicate the success of the program. So thoroughly indoctrinated is Offred that she admits enjoying taunting Janine, a victim of gang rape, and even succumbs to mass hysteria and takes an active role in a public execution. When a Japanese tour group tries to photograph Offred, she obscures her face behind her winged headgear and replies affirmatively to their question, "Are you happy?"

These instances suggest that Offred teeters on the brink of total acquiescence, a fact that haunts and terrifies her. Lacking the tough courage of a rebel, she keeps before her the examples of her mother and of Moira, both capable of razzing the establishment, of subverting authority. Offred lacks Moira's chutzpah, as demonstrated by the dismemberment of the toilet flusher for use as a weapon against Aunt Elizabeth, but Offred does possess a sense of humor that is similar to Moira's, a valuable buffer for some of her stolid moodiness and haunting dreams. Like some adults, Offred is approaching mid-life (roughly the age of Christ at the time of the Crucifixion) when she learns to value her mother's commitment to women's rights. A little like a sorrowful child herself, she looks back at her own daughter and dares hope that the child retains some memory of mother love.

Against the large screen on which Offred plays out her servitude are the lesser "Of's"—the first Ofglen, who maintains the dogma of Handmaidenhood during visits to the cemetery and past the Wall; the subsequent Ofglen, who whispers that her predecessor hanged herself; and Ofcharles, the nameless, story-less victim of a Salvaging. A strong "Of" is "Ofwarren," who retains enough of her former personality to be called Janine through most of the novel. A cloyingly complicitous trainee at Red Center, Janine annoys even the iron-spined Aunt Lydia with her ecstasy and cathartic reliving of gang rape. However, Atwood rescues Janine from the stereotype of the sycophant by revealing an early scene of mental derangement, followed by a head-forward, contraction-wracked birthing, and tears for little Angela, the handicapped infant whom she can never claim as her own. In the end, Janine/Ofwarren becomes Of-somebody else, but her mind ceases to observe rationality. Like a ubiquitous clerk or receptionist, she wishes her Handmaiden sisters to "have a nice day." To Offred, Janine, now "in free fall," is unsalvageable.

Clustered about Janine and the other breeders is the pecking order of Gilead womanhood: Wives, Daughters, Aunts, Marthas, Econowives, and Unwomen. Serena Joy is a composite drawn from Mirabel Morgan, Tammy Faye Bakker, and Phyllis Schlafly; she is the true turncoat against women and must live with her futile hope for a return to traditional womanhood. Her own television career curtailed, Serena now suffers the pain of arthritis as her joints, like her compassion, freeze up. Her hands, endlessly turning out geometrically cloned hominids on knitted wool scarves, reach for the effusive flowers that mock her sterility. Like Desdemona in Shakespeare's *Othello*, Serena associates herself with the willow, a gentle symbol of endless grief. Like Niobe, the weeping non-mother of Greek mythology, Serena has no choice but to support Offred in concubinage to the Commander and surreptitious couplings with Nick if the family is ever to produce a child.

THEMES

Central to *The Handmaid's Tale* is the failed attempt to produce **stasis** in the form of a one-dimensional, ultra-conservative society. Like the figures marching across Serena Joy's knitting or the Handmaids walking two by two to the meat market, Gilead's citizenry is the product of a fiasco: a mock factory system methodically installed to enforce traditional values—that is, the fundamentalist concept of godliness. Oddly, on all levels of this sterile, soulless theocracy, the dynamics of God play virtually no part. As a worshipper, the Commander locks away the family Bible, which he, as male family head, retrieves for a brief reading before the monthly mating ceremony. The only other worship outlet is the local computerized prayer scripting franchise, where phone-in orders result in "five different prayers: for health, wealth, a death, a birth, a sin." Atwood skewers this mechanized, voice-over performance by depicting the robotic Holy Rollers recycling paper print-outs.

To assure **consistency** in the populace, the hierarchy either annihilates or exiles those who fall outside Gilead's limited needs. For women who aren't capable of producing babies or of working as matron, indoctrinator, spouse, guard, or dray, the Colonies await, promising death from radiation poisoning. Likewise, males like the Commander, Nick, and street guards must fit the tight pattern of role expectation or else suffer the consequence. According to the

Twelfth Symposium, Commander Frederick Waterford is one of the many who fell short of the first cut. Judged too liberal, despite his contribution to the conservative regime, he disappears during a purge, an internal political cleansing that parallels abortion. Like a "shredder" baby, Waterford is disposed of in order to make way for an even more stringent Gilead.

Ironically, Gilead's attempts to root out nonwhites and dissidents fail. The terroristic cabal that wipes out the world of Luke and Offred, like the Puritanism of seventeenth-century New England, collapses, leaving behind enough shards of its quirky idiosyncrasies to make it an attractive focus for Professor Crescent Moon and Professor Pieixoto. Like a pterodactyl fallen from the sky and left to fossilize, Gilead precedes a period of multiculturalism, as evidenced by the names, nationalities, locale, and studies of dignitaries at the Twelfth Symposium of Gileadean Studies. A weak, hopeful sign is the name of Professor Maryann Crescent Moon, suggesting both rebel novelist Mary Ann Evans and a sliver of night light in the waxing stage, an eternal symbol of fecundity and womanly powers.

SETTING

Atwood draws settings evocative of a fast-paced shift of moods. By probing Offred's pensive moments in the quiet of her Byzantine cell or on languorous walks to town by way of the cemetery or river, the author balances ennui and too much introspection with unforseen moments of unpredictability. Without warning, Offred deserts a bland meal to enter the Birthmobile and hurry to the home of Commander Warren. At the side of Ofwarren, whose labor pains precede Aunt Elizabeth's assisted delivery of baby Angela, Offred witnesses one of the more pleasant moments in an otherwise bleak series of scenarios. As Handmaids chant encouragement, the Wives leave their banqueting and prepare Warren's Wife for the Birthing Stool, through which Ofwarren's child is born. Atwood saves for later the sobering fact that Angela turns out to be a "shredder," Gilead's cynical term for a freak, the product of radiation-damaged reproductive cells.

From the vivid birthing scene to a suspenseful night prowl of Commander Fred's parlor, Offred, lurking in the dark sitting room, is drawn into Nick's embrace, then acknowledges the bizarre message—her master wants to see her in his private quarters. Incapable of guessing what he might want with her—more passionate sex, perversion, maybe even torture—she is nonplussed to enter a Scrabble competition, calling on word talents she has almost lost through months of living without books or newspapers. With the agility of a born negotiator, Offred profits from the Commander's need for more intimacy and parlays her value to him into hand lotion and facts about the political scene.

From the privacy of "dates" in the den, Offred is startled to receive a showgirl's outfit, complete with makeup, heels, and cloak, and to find herself being whisked away to Jezebel's into a setting that, by Gilead's standards, no longer exists. The "meat market" bar scene, now frequented by Arab and Japanese businessmen, jolts Offred into the old-time man-woman games of flirtation, enticement, seduction, and acquiescence. Recalling that the nightclub was once a hotel, she pictures herself spending afternoons in clandestine meetings with Luke. Once more in a hotel bathroom, she must steady her nerve before performing the familiar female ritual of convincing her "date" of her eagerness to be seduced. To his dismay, she can only lie supine, a body obeying a mind that screams, "Fake it."

The last six chapters pick up the rhythm of scene change. From her lonely upstairs room, Offred escapes the stifling over-ripeness of summer and creeps downstairs to the kitchen with Serena Joy and outside to Nick's quarters. To Offred's guilt-ridden dismay, the covert sessions with the chauffeur draw her into repeated trysts. Like a foretaste of doom, a tolling bell summons Offred and the rest of the female population to a Salvaging and Particicution. So unnerved is the main character that she returns to her room in an irrational state. Smelling the tar that her hands have encountered on the rope, Offred responds to animal-like urgings—the need to clean her hands of death, intense hunger, and a cry of "*I am, I am*," like a wolf baying at the moon.

The familiar street scene in Chapter 44 yanks Offred further into mental trauma—Ofglen has evaded arrest by killing herself. Overwhelmed by the encroachment of Gilead's power, Offred is just beginning to calm herself when she encounters Serena and the incriminating sequined costume, proof that Offred and the Commander have transgressed Gilead's controlled mating ceremony. By night, Offred stares from the window and enumerates her choices, ranging from fire and murder to a plea for mercy to flight to an agonized suicide. In one quick scene, Nick and two escorts whisk her down the stairs, past the Commander and Serena Joy, and into the van, an ambiguous Hellmouth that could lead to freedom or a hook on the Wall.

A NOTE ON THE FILM VERSION OF
THE HANDMAID'S TALE

Filmed in Germany in 1990 for Cinecom, Director David Ray's version of Atwood's novel captures the desperation and duplicity of Gilead at the same time that it alters drastically the plot and style of the story. Some significant changes in the action include these:

- identity of Offred as Kate, a former librarian
- friendship with Moira begun at the Red Center rather than in college
- Offred and Moira's overpowering and trussing Aunt Lydia to a urinal
- bar-coded bracelets instead of tattoos for Handmaids, who wear veils rather than the white-winged wimples
- a mutually satisfying affair with Nick, who acknowledges that Offred's baby is his
- sound effects, particularly the cries of Kate's daughter Jill on the snowy hillside, ominous percussion during the roundup of blacks, and significant music, for example, "The Most Beautiful Girl in the World" during the presentation of Angela to the Wives
- car bombing
- theoretical identification of Commander Fred as head of Gilead's security
- a black dress and boa and feigned identification as Mary Lou for Offred's night out at Jezebel's
- Fred's rationalization that meeting clients at Jezebel's is good for business
- gloves on Moira's hands to conceal the effects of torture
- a luxury suite for Fred and Offred's clandestine copulation
- Offred's murder of the Commander with a knife supplied by Ofglen
- Fred eulogized by film clips on television news

• Nick's tender, but hasty separation from Kate as she is spirited away from Gilead

Most significant to the film's conclusion is the absence of the inal chapter, which is replaced by a brief glimpse of Kate, great vith child, in a rural setting, where she lives in a small trailer and iwaits messages from Nick.

REVIEW QUESTIONS AND ESSAY TOPICS

(1). Compare the dystopia of Gilead with the Oceania of George Orwell's *1984*, the futuristic London of Aldous Huxley's *Brave New World*, the California setting of Ray Bradbury's *Fahrenheit 451*, and the imprisoning world of Ayn Rand's *Anthem*. Enumerate characteristics and restrictions that repress, embitter, disenfranchise, and dishearten residents. Explain how Atwood builds on realities, such as funerals for fetuses, endangered whales, Islamic fanaticism, group therapy, IRA terrorism, surrogate motherhood, and other items from current events as well as product names such as Wordperfect, Joy, and Lydia Pinkham, in the creation of a satiric fantasy.

(2). Compare Offred to other traumatized, demoralized women in modern literature, especially Sethe in Toni Morrison's *Beloved*, Olivia Rivers in Ruth Prawar Jhabvala's *Heat and Dust*, young Jeanne in Jeanne Wakatsuki Houston's autobiographical *Farewell to Manzanar*, Janie in Zora Neale Hurson's *Their Eyes Were Watching God*, Yoko and Ko in Yoko Kawashima Watkins' *So Far from the Bamboo Grove*, the title character in William Styron's *Sophie's Choice*, and young Maya in Maya Angelou's autobiographical *I Know Why the Caged Bird Sings*.

(3). Discuss Margaret Atwood's distancing technique, which allows her to examine the dystopian microcosm of Gilead from the perspective of two centuries. Account for the time span between Offred's incarceration at the Commander's house and the Twelfth Symposium's study in 2195.

(4). Contrast Robert Duvall's role as the Commander in the 1990 film version of *The Handmaid's Tale* with his title role in *THX-*

1138, a 1970 dystopian cult classic. How does the capricious distribution of power affect both characters? Extend this study of power and subjugation to other dystopian films, especially *Fahrenheit 451, 1984, Lord of the Flies*, and *A Clockwork Orange*.

(5). Using *The Handmaid's Tale* as a model, compose extended definitions of dystopia, speculative or cautionary fiction, misogyny, feminism, repression, pun, parody, allusion, aphorism, euphemism, polemics, fundamentalism, zealotry, brainwashing, irony, wit, satire, thriller, science fiction, and the futuristic novel.

(6). Create a background study of Atwood's allusions to issues and events of the 1980s, especially anti-feminism, punk culture, jogging suits and fluorescent running shoes, rape prevention, feminist networking, the underground press, slogans and slang, pollution, anti-abortion violence, fetus burials, and Moral Majority politics.

(7). Study the stratification of female society in Gilead. Note the duties and significance of Unwomen, Wives, Daughters, Econowives, Handmaids, Marthas, and Aunts. Contrast the system's rigidity to the demands of Canadian and U.S. women in the 1980s. Apply terms such as sexual politics, postfeminism, conservative backlash, Mommy Track, Glass Ceiling, and pink-collar jobs.

(8). Compare the speaker's depiction of wartime upheaval with similar themes in films, novels, and autobiographies such as *The Morning After, The Hiding Place, The Endless Steppe, Plenty, Playing for Time, Farewell to Manzanar*, and *Lord of the Flies*. Emphasize the emotional and spiritual accommodations to trauma and repression that enable victims to survive.

(9). Discuss the role of underground support groups like Mayday. Contrast the coping mechanisms of Moira and Offred, particularly defiance, rebellion, escape, assertiveness, sexual indulgence, smoking, drugs, networking, and withdrawal.

(10). Apply to the well-ordered society Aunt Lydia's dictum: "There is more than one kind of freedom . . . freedom to and freedom from." In Gilead, what dividing lines separate freedom from fascism, patriotism from zealotry, duty from subservience, godliness from fanaticism?

(11). Discuss the use of ambiguity as an adjunct to irony and satire. How does Atwood balance ambiguity with epiphany, as in the discovery of a Latin inscription scratched in the closet wall or in Offred's departure in the van?

(12). Work out a section-by-section explanation of headings, especially "Household," "Birth Day," and "Soul Scrolls." Account for the repetition of "Night."

(13). Contrast the birth experience of Ofwarren with that of the central character in Atwood's 1977 short story, "Giving Birth," which is anthologized in Wendy Martin's short fiction collection, *We Are the Stories We Tell* (New York: Pantheon, 1990).

(14). Compare Atwood's bland, hypnotic tonelessness and claustrophobic tunnel vision with the control of the speaker in Jonathan Swift's *A Modest Proposal*. What do the two speakers gain by appearing to examine inhumanity from a dispassionate point of view?

(15). In an interview with Lindsy Van Gelder for *Ms.* in January 1987, Atwood called for an end to intolerant authoritarian groups—Puritans, Communists, Concerned Women of America—and the beginning of inclusive thinking. Debate Atwood's summary statement: "You have to draw lines; otherwise you're a total jellyfish. But please, let's start drawing *human* lines."

SELECTED BIBLIOGRAPHY

ATWOOD, MARGARET. "Cherished Moments," *Life*, Fall 1988, 153–58.

_____. "Comments," *University of Toronto Quarterly*, Spring 1992, 382.

_____. "Great Unexpectations," *Ms.* July/August 1987, 78–79, 195–196.

_____. "My Brother," *Harper's*, Mar. 1989, 36–38.

_____. "Summers on Canada's Rideau Canal," *Architectural Digest*, June 1988, 84–91.

_____. "Women's Novels," *Harper's*, May 1993, 32–33.

BERGMAN, HARRIET F. "Teaching Them to Read: A Fishing Expedition in *The Handmaid's Tale*," *College English*, December 1989, 847–54.

BLUESTEIN, GENE. "Storytellers," *Progressive*, September 1990, 40–42.

CAMPBELL, CHARLES. "Canada Becomes More Than a Writers' Novelty," *Chicago Tribune*, January 26, 1986, n.p.

Canadian Writers at Work: Interviews with Geoff Hancock. Toronto: Oxford University Press, 1987, 283–84.

Contemporary Authors New Revision Series. Volume 33. Detroit: Gale Research, 1989.

Contemporary Literary Criticism. Volume 44. Detroit: Gale Research, 1987.

DAVIDSON, CATHY N. "A Feminist *1984*," *Ms.*, February 1986, 24–26.

DREIFUS, CLAUDIA. "Margaret Atwood," *The Progressive*, March 1992, 30–33.

EHRENREICH, BARBARA. "Feminism's Phantoms," *New Republic*, March 17, 1986, 33–35.

GOTSCH-THOMSON, SUSAN. "The Integration of Gender into the Teaching of Classical Social Theory: Help from *The Handmaid's Tale*," *Teaching Sociology*, January 1990, 69–73.

GOULD, ALLAN M. "How Three Famous Women Cope with Success," *Chatelaine*, April 1988, 138–44.

GRAY, PAUL. "Repressions of a New Day," *Time*, February 10, 1986, 84.

HAMMER, STEPHANIE BARBÉE. "The World As It Will Be? Female Satire and the Technology of Power in *The Handmaid's Tale*," *Modern Language Studies*, Spring 1990, 39–49.

INGERSOLL, EARL G., ed. *Margaret Atwood: Conversations*. Princeton, N.J.: Ontario Review Press, 1991.

LARSON, JANET L. "Margaret Atwood and the Future of Prophecy," *Religion and Literature*, Spring 1989, 27–61.

_____. "Margaret Atwood's Testaments: Resisting the Gilead Within," *Christian Century*, May 20, 1987, 496–98.

LECKER, ROBERT, and JACK DAVID, eds. *Canadian Writers and Their Work*. Fiction Series, Volume 9. ECW Press, 1987.

LOVERSO, MARIO P. "Atwood's Moral Fables: The Limits of the Dialectical Imagination," *Carry On Bumping*, John Metcalf, ed. ECW Productions Services, 1989.

Major Twentieth-Century Writers. Detroit: Gale Research, 1990.

MALAK, AMIN. "Margaret Atwood's *The Handmaid's Tale* and the Dystopian Tradition," *Canadian Literature*, Spring 1987, 9–16.

MCCARTHY, MARY. "Breeders, Wives and Unwomen," *New York Times Book Review*, February 9, 1986, 1, 35.

MCCOMBS, JUDITH, ed. *Critical Essays on Margaret Atwood*. Critical Essays on World Literature Series. Boston: G. K. Hall, 1988.

MINER, MADONNE. "'Trust Me': Reading the Romance Plot in Margaret Atwood's *The Handmaid's Tale*," *Twentieth Century Literature*, Summer 1991, 148–68.

MOLLINS, CARL. "A Rich Talent for All Seasons," *Maclean's*, December 26, 1988, 34–35.

MURPHY, PATRICK D. "Reducing the Dystopian Distance: Pseudo-Documentary Framing in Near-Future Fiction." *Science Fiction Studies*, March 1990, 25–40.

O'BRIEN, TOM. "Siren's Wail," *Commonweal*, April 26, 1986, 251–53.

OLENDORF, DONNA, ed. *Bestsellers*. Detroit: Gale Research, 1989.

PRESCOTT, PETER S. "No Balm in This Gilead," *Newsweek*, February 17, 1986, 70.

ROBINSON, LILLIAN S. "Coming of Age in Toronto," *Nation*, June 5, 1989, 776–79.

ROSS, CATHERINE SHELDRICK, and CORY BIEMAN DAVIES. *Canadian Children's Literature*. Volume 42, 1986.

Short Story Criticism. Volume 2. Detroit: Gale Research, 1988.

Something About the Author. Volume 50. Detroit: Gale Research, 1988.

STEIN, KAREN F. "Margaret Atwood's *The Handmaid's Tale*: Scheherazade in Dystopia," *University of Toronto Quarterly*, Winter 1991–1992, 269–79.

STIMPSON, CATHARINE R. "The Atwood Woman," *Nation*, May 31, 1986, 764–67.

TIMSON, JUDITH. "Atwood's Triumph," *Maclean's*, October 3, 1988, 56–61.

UPDIKE, JOHN. "Expeditions to Gilead and Seegard," *New Yorker*, May 12, 1986, 118–126.

VAN GELDER, LINDSY. "Margaret Atwood," *Ms.*, January 1987, 48–50.

VANSPANCKEREN, KATHRYN, and JAN G. CASTRO, eds. *Margaret Atwood: Vision and Forms*. Carbondale: Southern Illinois University Press, 1988.

VEVAINA, COOMI S. "Forging a Canadian Identity," *World Press Review*, June 1988, 60.

_____. "Wastelands in This New Gilead: An Analysis of Margaret Atwood's *The Handmaid's Tale*," *Ambivalence: Studies in Canadian Literature*. New Delhi: Allied Publishers Ltd., 1990.

WEXLER, JOYCE. "The Handmaid's Tale," *America*, July 5, 1986, 16–17.

WHITTAKER, TED, ed. *The Writer's Union of Canada: A Directory of Members*. The Writer's Union of Canada, 1981.

NOTES

NOTES

Cliffs Notes

Absalom, Absalom!
The Aeneid
Agamemnon
Alice in Wonderland
All the King's Men
All the Pretty Horses
All Quiet on the Western Front
All's Well & Merry Wives
The American
American Poets of the 20th Century
American Tragedy
Animal Farm
Anna Karenina
Antony and Cleopatra
Aristotle's Ethics
As I Lay Dying
The Assistant
As You Like It
Autobiography of Benjamin Franklin
Autobiography of Malcolm X
The Awakening
Babbitt
Bartleby & Benito Cereno
The Bean Trees
The Bear
The Bell Jar
Beloved
Beowulf
Billy Budd & Typee
Black Boy
Black Like Me
Bleak House
Bless Me, Ultima
The Bluest Eye & Sula
Brave New World
Brothers Karamazov
Call of the Wild & White Fang
Candide
Canterbury Tales
Catch-22
Catcher in the Rye
The Chosen
Cliffs Notes on the Bible
The Color Purple
Comedy of Errors
Connecticut Yankee in King Arthur's Court
The Count of Monte Cristo
Crime and Punishment
The Crucible
Cry, the Beloved Country
Cyrano de Bergerac
Daisy Miller & Turn of the Screw
David Copperfield
Death of a Salesman
The Deerslayer
Diary of Anne Frank
Divine Comedy—I: Inferno
Divine Comedy—II: Purgatorio
Divine Comedy—III: Paradiso
Doctor Faustus
Dr. Jekyll and Mr. Hyde
Don Juan

Don Quixote
Dracula
Dream of the Red Chamber
Emerson's Essays
Emily Dickinson: Poems
Emma
Ethan Frome
Euripides' Electra & Medea
The Faerie Queene
Fahrenheit 451
Far from the Madding Crowd
A Farewell to Arms
Farewell to Manzanar
Fathers and Sons
Faulkner's Short Stories
Faust Pt. I & Pt. II
Federalist Papers
Flowers for Algernon
For Whom the Bell Tolls
Frankenstein
French Lieutenant's Woman
Giants in the Earth
The Giver
Glass Menagerie & A Streetcar Named Desire
Go Down, Moses
The Good Earth
Grapes of Wrath
Great Expectations
Great Gatsby
Greek Classics
Gulliver's Travels
Hamlet
Handmaid's Tale
Hard Times
Heart of Darkness and Secret Sharer
Hemingway's Short Stories
Henry IV, Part 1
Henry IV, Part 2
Henry V
House Made of Dawn
The House of Seven Gables
Huckleberry Finn
I Know Why the Caged Bird Sings
Ibsen's Plays I
Ibsen's Plays II
The Idiot
Idylls of the King
The Iliad
Invisible Man
Ivanhoe
Jane Eyre
Joseph Andrews
The Joy Luck Club
Jude the Obscure
Julius Caesar
The Jungle
Kafka's Short Stories
Keats & Shelley
King Lear
The Kitchen God's Wife
The Last of the Mohicans
Le Morte-d'Arthur
Leaves of Grass
Les Miserables
A Lesson Before Dying
Light in August

The Light in the Forest
Lord Jim
Lord of the Flies
Lord of the Rings
Lost Horizon
Lysistrata & Other Comedies
Macbeth
Madame Bovary
Main Street
The Mayor of Casterbridge
Measure for Measure
The Merchant of Venice
Middlemarch
A Midsummer Night's Dream
The Mill on the Floss
Moby-Dick
Moll Flanders
Mrs. Dalloway
Much Ado About Nothing
Mutiny on the Bounty
My Ántonia
Mythology
Narrative of the Life of Frederick Douglass
Native Son
New Testament
Night
1984
Notes from the Underground
The Odyssey
Oedipus Trilogy
Of Human Bondage
Of Mice and Men
The Old Man and the Sea
Old Testament
Oliver Twist
One Day in the Life of Ivan Denisovich
One Flew Over the Cuckoo's Nest
100 Years of Solitude
O'Neill's Plays
Othello
Our Town
The Ox-Bow Incident
Paradise Lost
A Passage to India
The Pearl
The Pickwick Papers
The Picture of Dorian Gray
Pilgrim's Progress
The Plague
Plato's Euthyphro, Apology, Crito, & Phaedo
Plato's The Republic
Poe's Short Stories
A Portrait of the Artist as a Young Man
Portrait of a Lady
The Power and the Glory
Pride and Prejudice
The Prince
The Prince and the Pauper
A Raisin in the Sun
The Red Badge of Courage
The Red Pony
The Return of the Native
Richard II

Richard III
The Rise of Silas Lapham
Robinson Crusoe
Roman Classics
Romeo and Juliet
The Scarlet Letter
A Separate Peace
Shakespeare's Comedies
Shakespeare's Histories
Shakespeare's Minor Plays
Shakespeare's Sonnets
Shakespeare's Tragedies
Shaw's Pygmalion & Arms and the Man
Silas Marner
Sir Gawain and the Green Knight
Sister Carrie
Slaughterhouse-Five
Snow Falling on Cedars
Song of Solomon
Sons and Lovers
The Sound and the Fury
Steppenwolf & Siddhartha
The Stranger
The Sun Also Rises
T.S. Eliot's Poems & Plays
A Tale of Two Cities
The Taming of the Shrew
Tartuffe, Misanthrope & Th
Bourgeoise Gentleman
The Tempest
Tender Is the Night
Tess of the D'Urbervilles
Their Eyes Were Watching God
Things Fall Apart
The Three Musketeers
To Kill a Mockingbird
Tom Jones
Tom Sawyer
Treasure Island & Kidnapp
The Trial
Tristram Shandy
Troilus and Cressida
Twelfth Night
Ulysses
Uncle Tom's Cabin
The Unvanquished
Utopia
Vanity Fair
Vonnegut's Works
Waiting for Godot
Walden
Walden Two
War and Peace
Who's Afraid of Virginia Woolf?
Winesburg, Ohio
The Winter's Tale
The Worldly Philosophers
Wuthering Heights
A Yellow Raft in Blue Wate

Cliffs
NOTE

CPSIA information can be obtained at www.ICGtesting.com
Printed in the USA
BVOW07s2007270614

357605BV00001B/101/P